THE 1988
alternative
BOOK OF
RECORDS

THE 1988
alternative
BOOK OF
RECORDS

Mike Barwell

Drawings by Wilf Lunn

GRAFTON BOOKS
A Division of the Collins Publishing Group

LONDON GLASGOW
TORONTO SYDNEY AUCKLAND

Grafton Books
A Division of the Collins Publishing Group
8 Grafton Street, London W1X 3LA

Published by Grafton Books 1987

British Library Cataloguing in Publication Data

The Alternative book of records.—1988–
    1. World Records—Periodicals
    032′.02   AG240

ISBN 0-246-13264-7

Photoset by CG Graphic Services, Tring, Herts
Printed in Great Britain by
Robert Hartnoll (1985) Ltd, Bodmin

CONTENTS

Preface   vii

1. Outrageous Achievements   1

2. Collecting   67

3. Gastronomic Records   77

4. The Amazing Wilf Lunn   92

5. Sporting Records   97

6. That's Entertainment?   116

7. Pub Games and Pastimes   126

8. 'The Alternative Olympics'   133

Acknowledgements   136

Note

Some of the records reported in this book have involved the exercise of great skill and ingenuity. No one who has not received training or is not properly supervised should undertake any stunts which involve any degree of danger.

PREFACE

When I first started collecting scraps of information from media sources, back in the mid-sixties, little did I realise the potential value and importance of my hobby. Had I not kept updating and cross-referencing the bizarre trivia – even though much time was spent abroad in the Merchant Navy – the basis for *The Alternative Book of Records* might never have been realised.

Now *The Alternative Book of Records* is the acknowledged leader of reference books for the bizarre, inane, eccentric, and just plain mad feats which people perform for fame and self-satisfaction. But bear in mind one thing as you scour these pages. Many of the record-breakers featured have not only gained permanent recognition for themselves, they have helped to raise millions of pounds for charity and in so doing have contributed, in their own special way, to helping people less fortunate than themselves.

The *1988 Alternative Book of Records* has over 50 per cent more new and updated records. If you think you deserve more permanent recognition for your record-breaking feats, write to me, care of: Grafton Books, 8 Grafton Street, London W1X 3LA.

Mike Barwell

Chapter One

OUTRAGEOUS ACHIEVEMENTS

Aeroplane pulling

The shortest recorded time for pulling a 77 tonne Concorde aeroplane, using only muscle power and strong ropes, for a distance of 880 yards, is 32 min 17 sec by a team of 200 at Duxford Airfield, Cambridge, on 6 February 1983.

Airline ticket

The longest airline ticket ever issued was one measuring 39 ft 4 in, to Bruno Leunen at Brussels Airport, Belgium on 19 December 1984. The ticket was valid on 80 different airline companies for the 53,200 miles round the world trip which involved some 109 airports.

Aquatic ladder balancing

On 14 February 1949 J. Anthony Johnson of Cedar Rapids, Iowa, USA, swam a distance of 25 yards on his back whilst balancing a six foot ladder on his chin.

Army – smallest

The European country of Andorra boasts the world's smallest army. The full complement comprises one officer, six privates and four general staff. Its entire defence budget amounts to just three pounds which is spent on blank ammunition for ceremonial purposes.

Baby – the first American

On 18 August 1587 at Roanoke Island the first non-Indian child was born of English parents. Virginia Dare was the daughter of Elizabeth and John Dare, who had settled in America as part of a 150 strong group of colonists transported from England by Sir Walter Raleigh.

Backgammon

The longest session of Backgammon ever recorded was by Richard T. Newcomb and Greg Peterson of Rockford, Illinois, USA, from 30 June to 6 July 1978, a total of 151 hours.

Balancing

Stanley Reid, 20, of Stranraer, Scotland, balanced unsupported on one leg atop a stack of 12 ten pence pieces for a period of one minute on 18 June 1984.

Ball balancing

Amateur soccer player David Naylor of Aylesbury, Bucks, jogged 200 yards in the record time of 49.6 seconds whilst balancing a football in the pit of his neck on 29 May 1985.

Balloon bursting

Jane Rowlands and Mary Smith, both aged 12 of Andover, Hampshire, burst 1,000 air-filled balloons, held in a 20 ft by 8 ft cargo container, using only hands, feet and body in a time of 26 min 30 sec on 20 August 1977.

Balloon – long distance

A balloon released by Justin Fiorey on 19 April 1982 from Dobbs Ferry, New York State, USA, landed in Wagga Wagga, Australia, 11 months later on 21 February 1983 after covering a distance of some 10,000 miles.

Bankrupt

The World's biggest bankrupt is Rajendra Sethia, head of the Esal Commodities Co. He was declared bankrupt in the High Court in London in January 1985 with debts of £170 million.

Barge pulling

On 5 August 1985, Reg Morris of Brownhills, West Midlands, towed an 80 tonne barge 880 yards from the Red Iron Bridge to the Royal Oak public house along the Pelsall canal, using only his teeth, in the record breaking time of 6 min 10 sec.

There was a time when the humble bath was reserved for the more personal traditions of hygiene. However, apart from now racing with them and using them to sail around Europe, people are filling their baths with the oddest things.

Bath of baked beans

The longest recorded time for a sit-in in a bath of cold baked beans is 100 hours by Barry (Captain) Kirk of Port Talbot, West Glamorgan. Barry's 'Beanathon' was staged at the Aberfan Hotel, between 11 and 15 September 1986.

Bath of custard

Drama student Helen Coleman laid claim to a new world record for sitting in a bath of custard. Starting at Hull's

3

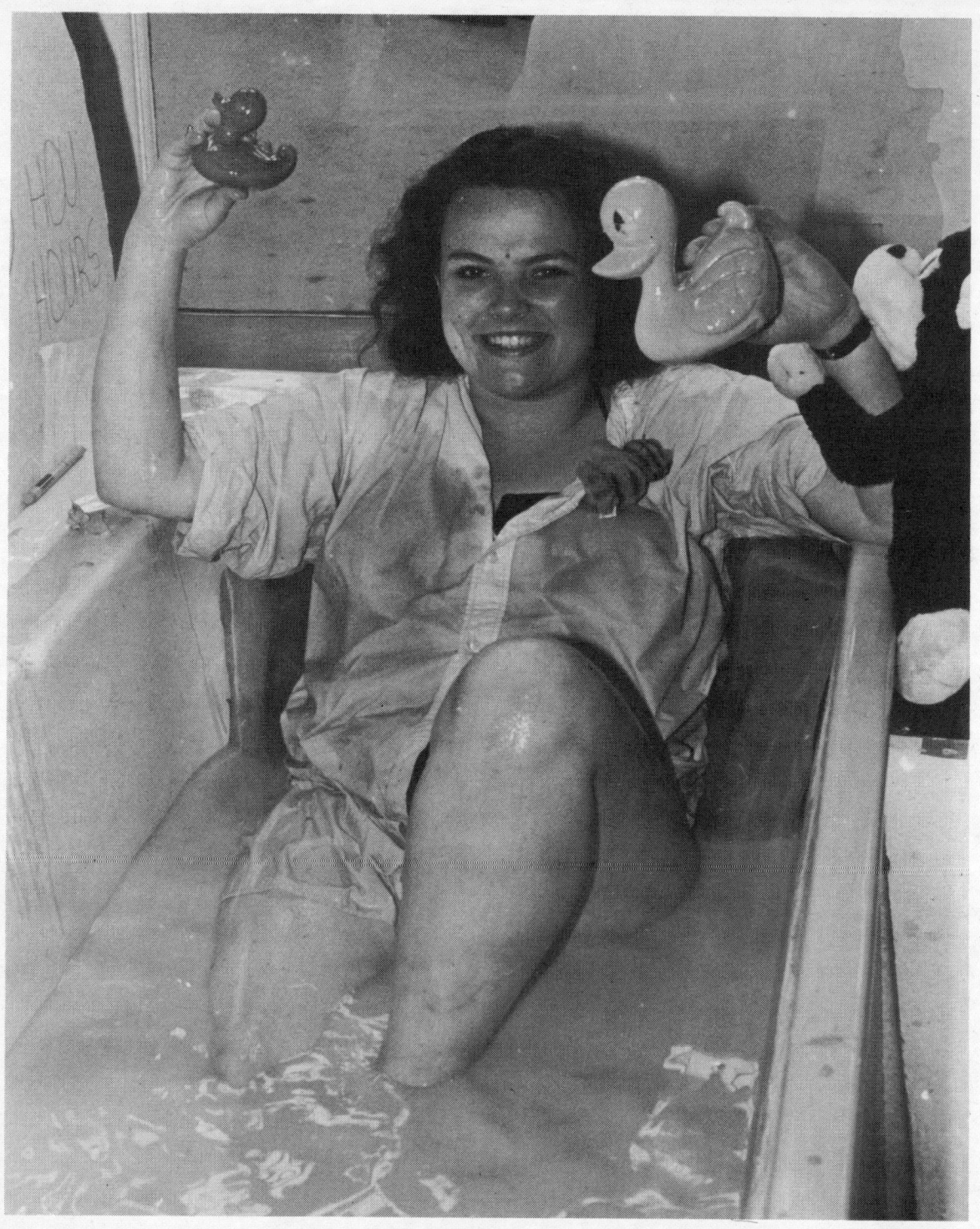

Paragon Station on 19 June 1986, Helen's ordeal finished 42 hours later at Beverley Gala on 20 June 1986.

Bath of maggots

Probably the most unsavoury of 'bath sits' ever completed was one of 24 hours in a bath containing over two million maggots. The feat was accomplished by Peter Smart at The Goldfinger Tavern, Highworth, Wiltshire, from 10 to 11 August 1985.

Bath of milk

As a protest at cutbacks in EEC subsidies, 20 bikini-clad wives and daughters of Welsh dairy farmers took a 30 minute bath in 300 gallons of fresh milk in the middle of the town centre at Carmarthen, Wales, on 16 May 1984.

Bath of porridge

Starting on 7 June 1986 at Birmingham's National Exhibition

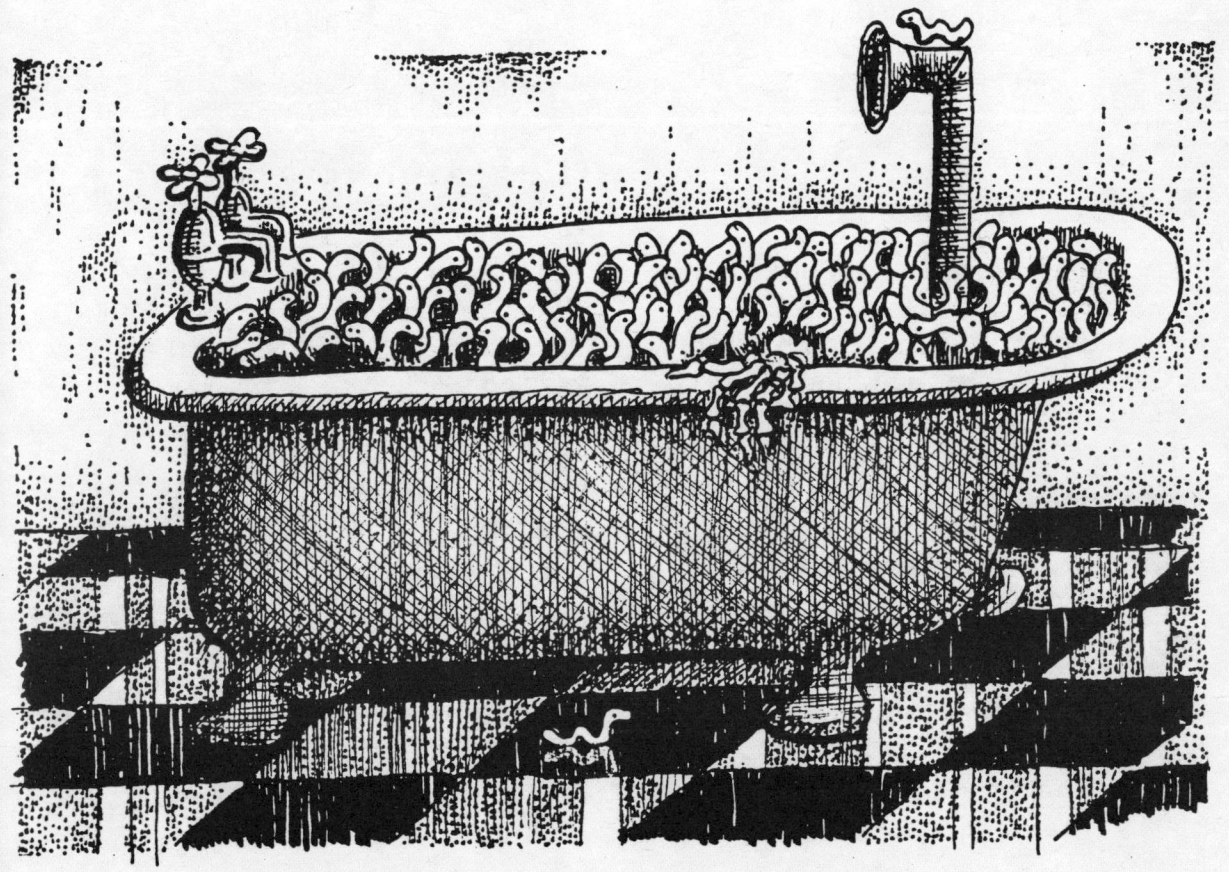

Centre, Roger Jones, 42, of Redditch, Worcs, sat in a bath of cold porridge for the record time of 80 hr 36 min. During the marathon, which ended on 10 June 1986, Roger was towed the 20 miles back to his local pub in Redditch where the 90 gallons of porridge were donated to the inmates at Roger's place of work – the local 'nick'.

Bath racing

Using an assortment of trolley-mounted bath tubs, a group of students from Hobart, Tasmania, staged a 10-mile bath tub race from Hobart to Claremont on 17 June 1983. The winners, with a time of 4 hr 6 min 52 sec, were Chris Durban and Dave Turpin (pushers) and Sue Cockroft (bather).

Bath of spaghetti

Rob Gordon, 24, of Shrewsbury, Shropshire, sat in a bath of spaghetti for an incredible 360 hours, starting on 21 September 1984 and finishing on 6 October 1984. The bath was mounted on a wheeled trolley so that Rob could be pushed around the streets of Shrewsbury and also carry out his duties as a disc jockey during the evenings.

Bath tub sailor

On 9 October 1983, Bill Neal of Salcombe, Devon, completed a 1,800 mile sail from London to Korkta, Finland, in a fibreglass, jacuzzi-type bath tub accompanied by three friends in a support boat. Bill's journey took almost four months to complete.

Bed – most expensive

The most expensive bed ever sold was a 1930 example of a king-size 'Jean Durand', auctioned at Christie's, New York, USA on 2 October 1983 for £49,668.

Bed cramming

Sixty-eight staff and regulars at The Warehouse public house in Hertford, Herts, set a new world record on 19 October 1984, by piling into the same iron-framed bed.

Bed of glass – duration

The duration record for lying on a bed of broken glass is 72 hr 30 min by Reg Morris from 1 to 4 April 1985 at 'Jumbo Discount Stores', Darleston, West Midlands.

Bed of glass – greatest weight

On 13 February 1982, Barry Silver of Manchester lay on a bed of broken glass with a 2,100 lb weight spread evenly over a board on his chest.

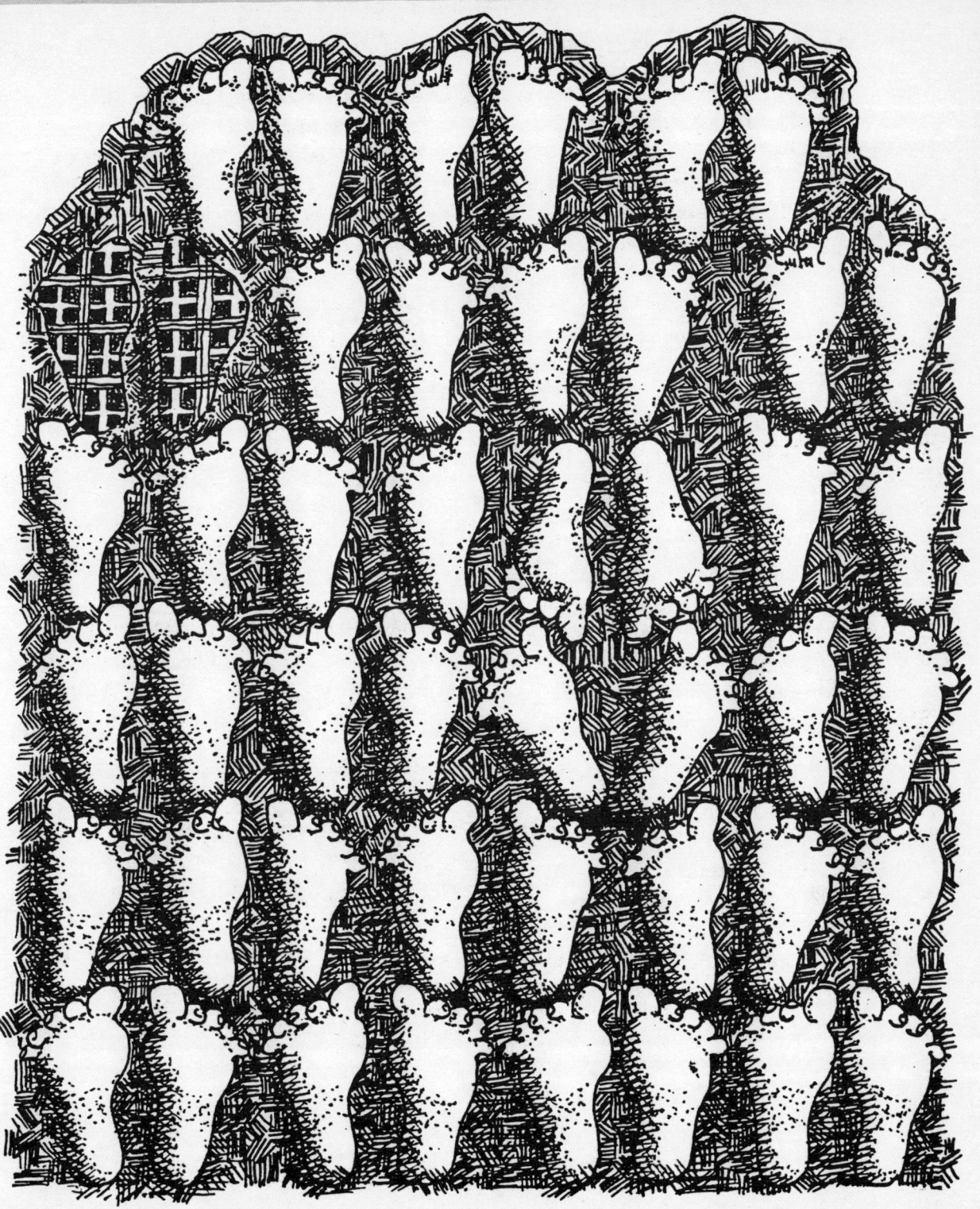

Bed of nails – duration

The duration record for lying on a bed of unblunted six-inch nails is held by Reg Morris of Walsall, West Midlands. Between 2 and 15 October 1984 at the Sportsman Inn, Brownhills, West Midlands, he lay non-stop on a bed of nails for exactly 310 hours.

Bed of nails – greatest weight

On BBC Television's 'Late Late Breakfast Show' on 10 December 1983 John Kassar lay prone on a bed of unblunted six-inch nails. A wooden board was placed on his chest and 29 girls climbed on to it. The total weight pressing down on John's body was 1 ton 12 cwt 3 st 12 lb (3,638 lb). Although his body was marked, the sharp nails did not penetrate the skin.

Bed race

The fastest recorded time for completing the annual Knaresborough Bed Race is 12 min 36 sec by 'The Beavers' team on 9 June 1984. Held annually in North Yorkshire, the bed race course crosses the River Nidd and is just over two miles in length.

Bed of swords

The greatest recorded time for lying across the sharpened blades of four military swords is 32 hours, by Reg Morris, from 12 to 13 September 1984, at The Castle Club, Brownhills, West Midlands.

Beer crate racing

At the 'Alternative Olympics', Hull, on 31 August 1986, Paul Smith from Brentwood, Essex, set a new world record for the 500 metre beer crate race of 1 min 31.7 sec.

Beer crate stacking

Using standard plastic beer crates, Brian McMahon, Brendan Donnelly and Ian Watson stacked 22 crates in a 25 ft high column at Scunthorpe, Humberside, on 29th July 1978.

Beer glass lifting

On 9 January 1987, Mr Geoffrey Prest, the landlord of The Black Horse Inn, Roos, Humberside, lifted 21 pint glasses full of ale without handles.

The record for lifting pint glasses full of ale, with handles, is held by Walter Cornelius (d. 1983), who lifted 30 at the Dolphin Inn, Peterborough, Cambs, on 20 September 1971.

Bench weight

The greatest weight ever supported by a human being, across his chest, with one bench supporting the head and another the feet, is 55 st 10 lb (780 lb) by Fred Burton of Cheadle, Staffordshire, on 7 April 1981. The plank placed across Fred's chest was weighted by six members of the 'Cheadle Charmers' dance group.

Bible reading

Over the Easter period of 1981, ten youngsters from the Ashby Wesley Methodist Church, Scunthorpe, Humberside, read the entire Bible from the pulpit, covering 773,106 words in the record time of 69 hr 33 min.

Bicycle – world's largest

The largest bicycle ever built was completed on 2 July 1984 by Kesashichiro Tagawa of Osaka, Japan at a cost of £7,000. The 5 metre long, 3.4 metre high bicycle took over three years to build. Mr Tagawa is now looking for a volunteer to try to ride the thing!

Bigamy

On 31 December 1981, Florida police issued a statement to the effect that Giovanni Vigliotto had admitted to no less than 82 bigamous marriages dating back to 1949. By the time he was brought to trial on 1 February 1983, Vigliotto, then aged 53, confessed to the Phoenix, Arizona, court that he had in fact married no less than 115 times, including four times in the space of three weeks whilst cruising the Caribbean with a friend in 1968. On 28 March 1983, he was sentenced to 28 years imprisonment and fined $336,000.

Bog squatting

The longest recorded bog squat is one of 4 hr 39 min by Frank Cartin, landlord of

'The White Horse' public house, Bootham, York on 28 March 1986. Contestants must remain seated, without trousers or undergarments, at all times.

The clothed bog squatting record is held by Simon Hayhurst, 20, with a time of 5 hr 1 min at the 'Sacks of Potatoes', Birmingham, on 3 April 1986.

Bond signing

On 22 September 1978, Salvation Army Major, George D. Thomas, signed 12,551 specially prepared charity bonds in 16 hr 30 min outside a supermarket in Hull, Humberside. The bonds were on sale to the general public and George raised £138.50 for his chosen charity.

Boomerang throwing

On 7 April 1984, at Albert, New South Wales, Australia, Robert Croll successfully completed 653 consecutive throws and catches of his competition boomerang.

Bottle opening octopus

'Oliver', the pet octopus belonging to 19-year-old Nicholas Kruger of Port Elizabeth, South Africa, broke his own world record on 21 December 1985, by uncorking a bottle in 12.82 seconds. As an incentive, the bottles contained tasty young crabs – Oliver's favourite food.

Brick carrying

The holder of the marathon brick carrying record is Reg Morris of Brownhills, West Midlands. On 26 July 1985, Reg carried a 9 lb Staffordshire brick a distance of 61¾ miles from Oswestry to Brownhills in a time of exactly 13 hours. The brick must be carried in the same ungloved hand in a downward position.

Not to be outdone by her extrovert husband, Mrs Wendy Morris smashed the female brick carrying record on 28 April 1987, when she carried a 9 lb 6 oz brick 22½ miles on a round trip from Brownhills to Cannock, West Midlands, in 5 hr 35 min.

Brick lifting

The greatest number of 8 in × 4 in × 2½ in building bricks ever lifted in the clamp position is 26, by Alan Keates of Cheadle, Staffs, on 15 May 1984. The total weight lifted was 130 lbs.

Brick throwing

At Braybook School Gala, Orton, Goldhay, Cambridgeshire, on 19 July 1978, Geoff Capes (now the world's strongest man) threw a 5 lb building brick 146 ft 1 in.

Brownie – oldest

The oldest person to join the Brownies was Helen Moss of Bicester, Oxfordshire, who at the age of 86 was admitted to her first pack on 9 October 1983.

Bubble

The biggest bubble ever made without the aid of mechanical contrivances was produced by Katherine Harting on BBC TV's 'Show Me How' on 14 September 1983. Using only a piece of wire bent into a circular shape and a strong solution of soap suds, Katherine

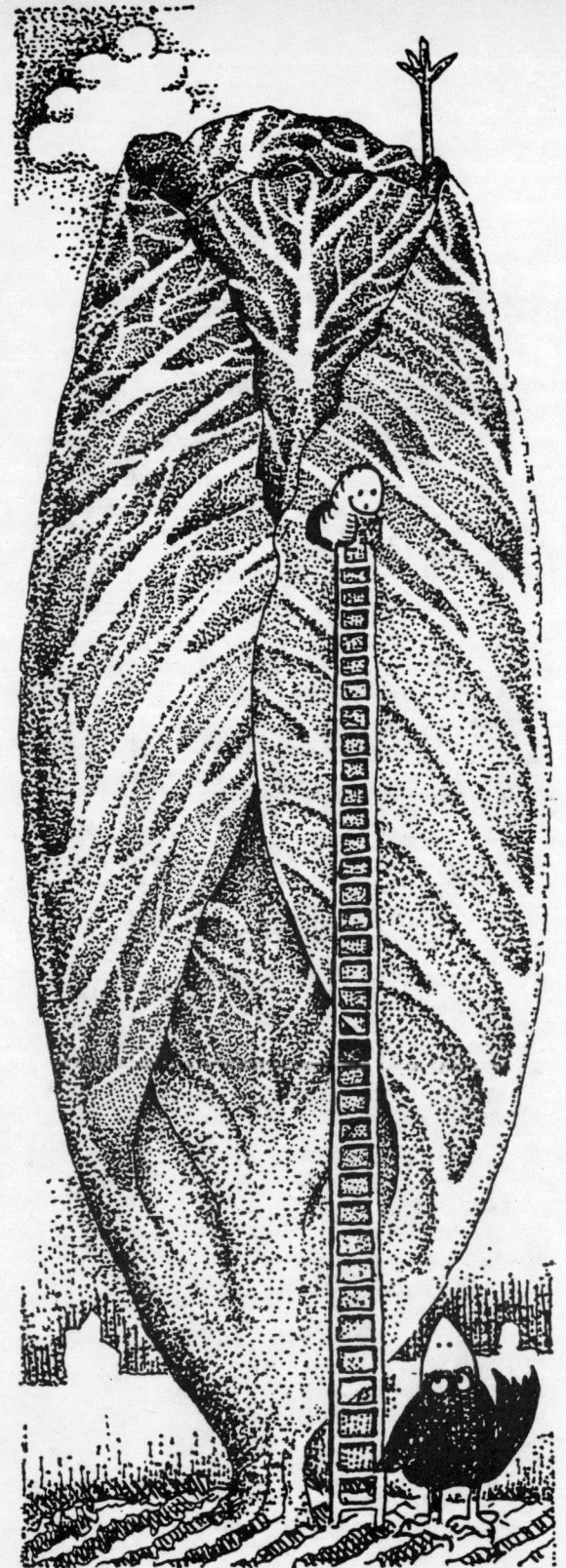

produced the mammoth 46.8 cm diameter bubble.

Bubble gum blowing

The largest bubble ever blown using bubble gum is one measuring 55.8 cm in diameter by Susan Montgomery of Fresno, California, USA, on 31 June 1985. The joint British and European record holders are 18-year-old Nigel Fell of Derriaghy, Northern Ireland, and 16-year-old John Smith of Willingham, Cambridgeshire, who have both blown bubbles measuring 42 cm in diameter.

Bus jumping

The greatest number of double-decker buses cleared by a motorcyclist is 18. The feat was achieved by 25-year-old Chris Brownham at Bromley, Kent on 29 August 1983.

Bus pushing

Using only his head, Walter Cornelius pushed a double decker bus half a mile in the time of 15 min 17 sec on 14 September 1972 at Peterborough, Cambridgeshire.

Cabbages

The tallest cabbage ever grown was of the Jersey variety, reared by John Black of Milnthorpe, Lancaster, Lancashire. On 7 May 1983 the monster had reached 13 ft 6½ in in height.

The largest and heaviest cabbage ever grown was one weighing 123 lb by Bill Collingwood of Swalwell, County Durham, exhibited on 4 September 1965.

Cage of snakes

Reptile expert Juergen Hegert completed a 100 day incarceration in a glass cage full of poisonous snakes, ending on 24 August 1986. The feat, performed in Gulf Breeze, Florida, USA, unfortunately had a sad ending – his girlfriend got fed up with waiting for him and ran off with another man.

Canal jumping

The only person ever to perfect the art of canal jumping was Billy Barker of Manchester (died 14 March 1965 aged 84).

Carrying a 25 lb 'balance weight' in each hand, Bill would leap from a canal bank. As his feet touched the water he would thrust the weights upwards with such force that he was propelled into the air again and up on to the opposite bank. The widest canal that super-fit Billy jumped by this method was 17 ft wide.

Candle – biggest

The largest candle ever constructed was completed on 1 June 1986 at Tegelan, Holland. Sixty-eight members of Tegelan Athletics Club worked for eight days to complete the 89 ft monster.

Cannon ball pushing

On 1 March 1986 Reg Morris pushed a cannon ball (a 16 lb shot) using only his nose around Walsall, West Midlands, for a distance of one mile in exactly 42 minutes.

Cannons

Queen Christina of Sweden had a morbid hatred of fleas. In 1632 she ordered a miniature cannon to be built measuring just 4 inches long. It was kept charged and loaded with minute shot and sited in her private chambers. Whenever she saw a flea she would fire the cannon and blow it to pieces, together with whatever the insect was sitting on.

The largest cannon ever to be fired was one used by the Turkish militia in 1453. Its overall length was 36 ft 6 in and it weighed 42 tonnes. The stone cannon balls each weighed approximately 2,100 lb.

Cans – largest pyramid

The world's biggest pyramid of tin cans was constructed at Maizuru Playground, Nagoya, Japan, between 3 and 4 November 1985. 210,479 empty cans were used in the completed pyramid which was built to celebrate the International Youth Year.

Car and bus cramming

These car and bus cramming records are all subject to the following rules:

The vehicle must be a standard production model.
No seats, fitments and such shall be removed.
All windows, doors, boot and bonnet must be closed on completion.
The time limit to achieve the record must be no more than 10 minutes.

The BL Metro record stands at 21, achieved by members of the Plymouth Young Wives Association at Devonport, Devon, on 30 September 1982.

The Ford Escort record stands at 20, set by students of Birmingham University on 16 November 1985.

The Ford Sierra record is 27, achieved by students at the University of Nottingham on 14 October 1985.

The record for the Jaguar XJ6 is 42, set by The Moss Bay Majorettes at Jacksonville, Florida, USA, on 26 August 1984.

The Volkswagen Beetle record is 34, set by members of Chelsea College, Eastbourne, Sussex, on 15 February 1969.

The greatest number of people to cram on to a standard 56-seater double-decker bus is 196 at Patrington Haven Caravan Park, Patrington, North Humberside, on 13 July 1986.

Car and caravan jump

Frenchman Gerard Stoeckli achieved a new world record distance of 75 ft.whilst clearing 15 parked cars with his own car which was towing a 14 ft caravan. The jump might have been somewhat shorter had the caravan not landed on top of the towing car which somersaulted in the air.

Car jumping

The only man able to leap lengthways over two sports cars travelling at 100 mph is American Steve Lewis.

Following a horrific accident in April 1983, when Steve had his left foot ripped off, he finally succeeded in June 1984.

Car jump – longest attempted

The longest jump ever attempted in a four-wheel vehicle was by the American stunt-driver Ken Powers. In his ultra-tuned fuel injected 1976 Lincoln Continental, Ken attempted to jump the one mile distance from Morrisburg, Ontario, Canada, across the St Lawrence River to Ogden Island, USA. The site and specially built take-off ramp took over four years to prepare, involving the movement of 110,000 cubic yards of earth. The car left the ramp at a speed of 280 mph and soared (momentarily) to a height of 305 ft before a safety parachute prematurely opened causing the car to partially disintegrate in mid-air and plummet into the river. Fortunately, Ken was rescued by an emergency stand-by team and escaped serious injury.

Car lifting

Belgian strong-man, John Massis, claims to have the strongest teeth in the world and on several occasions has proved it.

On 4 February 1986 on Belgium's BRT TV-1, John lifted a 2,000 kg Opel car and driver 20 cm off the floor and held it aloft whilst the supporting scaffold was wheeled five metres forward.

Car pulling – female

The female record for uphill car pulling (gradient not less than 1 in 7) is 1 hr 9 min 31 sec by a team of 30 who pulled a 16 cwt vehicle for three miles up the Kirkstone Pass, Cumbria, on 20 July 1986.

Car top skiing

Firmly strapped to the specially strengthened roof rack atop a Ford Cosworth Sierra driven by his brother Graham, Stuart Wilkie of Guildford, Surrey, endured the greatest speed ever recorded, of 134.6 mph at Bruntingthorpe Proving Ground, Leicester, on 30 November 1986.

Caravan

The largest and most luxurious caravan ever built was completed on 20 October 1985 by the Newport Pagnell, Buckinghamshire firm, CSC (Specialised Vehicles) Ltd.

The caravan – one of four – was built specially for a Saudi Arabian prince and is 84 ft in length and weighs 35 tonnes. A ten-wheeled tractor will move it from site to site.

Each van is fully air-conditioned and every room has its own temperature control. There's double-glazing, solar-reflecting tinted glass, TV, video, hi-fi, a long-range telecommunication system, intercoms, and every bathroom has a jacuzzi. All the caravans will have hydraulic stabilisers to keep them on an even keel when the going gets rough in the desert. The price? A cool £260,000 each.

Card signing

Salvation Army Major George D. Thomas signed 9,000 cards in aid of charity in a 12 hour session on 25 June 1977 at Holywood Arches, Belfast, Northern Ireland.

Cat – most travelled

'Hamlet' – the stowaway cat – travelled 25 times round the world in the hold of a British Airways 747 Jumbo Jet. Hamlet began his marathon trip in Toronto, Canada, as an official passenger, but he had vanished from his cage by the time the aircraft arrived at Heathrow. He was finally found 6 weeks later on 16 April 1984, having survived on condensation water, during which time the aircraft had covered over 600,000 miles.

Catalogue tearing

On 19 October 1986, Geoff Fowler of Ledbury, Worcestershire, ripped in half a 1,000 page mail order catalogue in the record time of 9 min 12 sec.

Cement bag carrying

The greatest distance that two 1 cwt bags of cement have been carried (in this instance, balanced on the head) is 880 yards in 10 min 12 sec by Walter Cornelius of Peterborough on 17 March 1968.

Chair jumping

Insurance boss John Baker of Cheltenham, Gloucestershire raised £400 for cancer research in setting a new world record by leaping over a dining chair 22 times in a minute.

Champagne cork

According to reliable information, the greatest measured distance for the flight of a champagne cork – to final rest – is an incredible 116 ft 7½ in claimed by David Thorben, 21, at Newark, New Jersey USA on 6 September 1985.

Champagne fountain

On 19 April 1983, Carl Groves broke his own world record for stacking and filling champagne glasses. Carl and a willing assistant successfully filled 23 champagne glasses, stacked one on top of the other, at Richmond, Victoria, Australia.

Chest weight

On 6 June 1983, at Los Angeles, California, Yogi Pandi supported the weight of Debi, a 3 tonne Indian elephant, on a board placed across his chest.

Christmas pudding

Thursday 29 November 1984 should have been a momentous day for the villagers of Cottingham, North Humberside. For this was to be the day they completed baking the world's largest Christmas pudding. However, as the monster 200 lb pudding was being turned out, it split and collapsed into a steaming gooey mass of raisins, almonds, flour and spice.

Christmas tree

The world's tallest Christmas tree was a 221 ft Douglas Fir erected in a Seattle, Washington, USA, shopping centre in December 1950. The tallest Christmas tree ever erected in Great Britain was an 85 ft 3¼ in Norwegian Spruce on the South Bank, London, in November 1975.

Cigar

It would take about five years non-stop puffing to smoke the world's largest cigar.

Manufactured from 33,300 tobacco leaves by Tinus Vinke and Jan Weijmer in February 1983, and weighing 577 lb 9 oz, the 16 ft 8¼ in monster is housed in the Tobacco Museum at Kampen, Holland.

Cigars – most in mouth

On 30 September 1986, Andy Walters, 21, broke his own world record for cigar stuffing at the MF Snooker Centre, Hull, by cramming 28 full-sized Castella Cigars into his mouth.

Climbing

On 24 September 1985, a record-breaking 'climbathon' was completed by two soldiers from the First Battalion, King's Own Royal Border Regiment and three civilians from Great Eccleston, Lancashire, when they successfully climbed all 348 English peaks over 2,000 ft in height. Their achievement took 21 days and involved walking 425 miles.

Coal sack carrying

The world Coal Sack Carrying championships are held annually at Gawthorpe, Wakefield, Yorkshire, over a 1,000 metre course. The current record holder is 36-year-old Terry Lyons who humped the 1 cwt sack around the course in 4 min 19 sec on 16 April 1979.

The oldest person to complete the course was 69-year-old George Crossland on 29 March 1986.

Coconut smashing

Karate expert Mick Gouch smashes coconuts like other people smash eggs. The best times Mick has recorded are two smashed in 3.8 seconds and three smashed in 6.2 seconds.

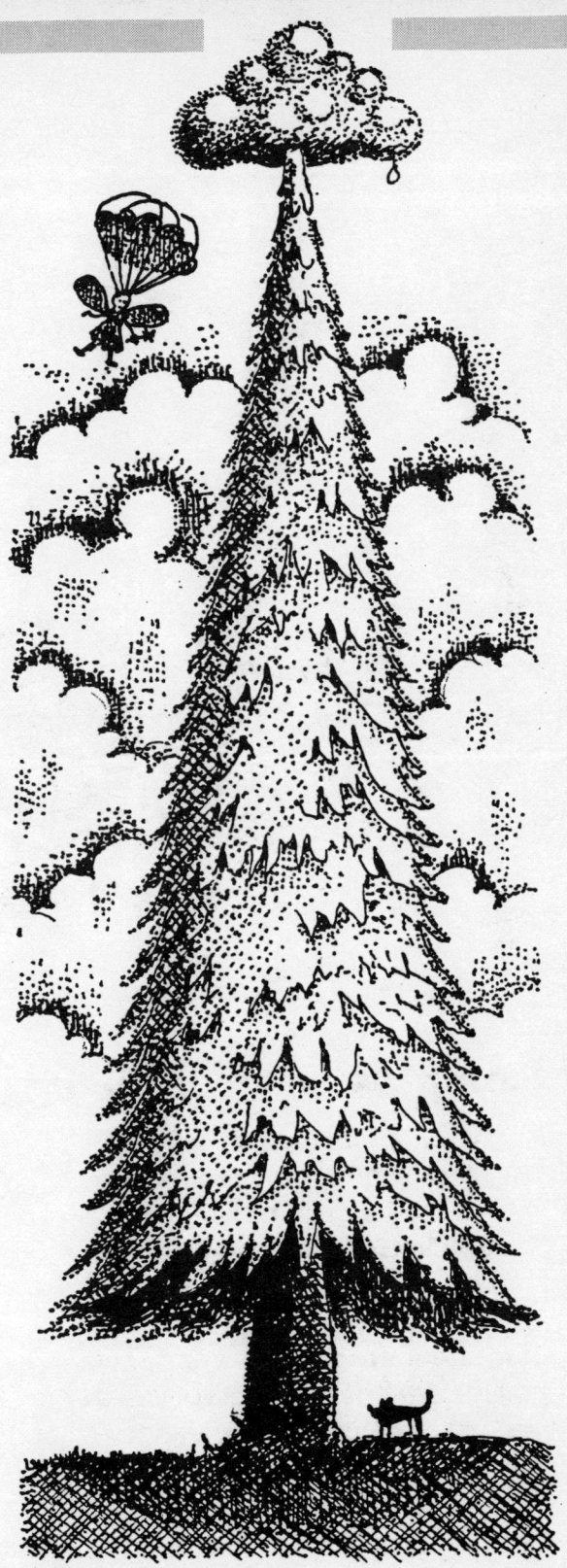

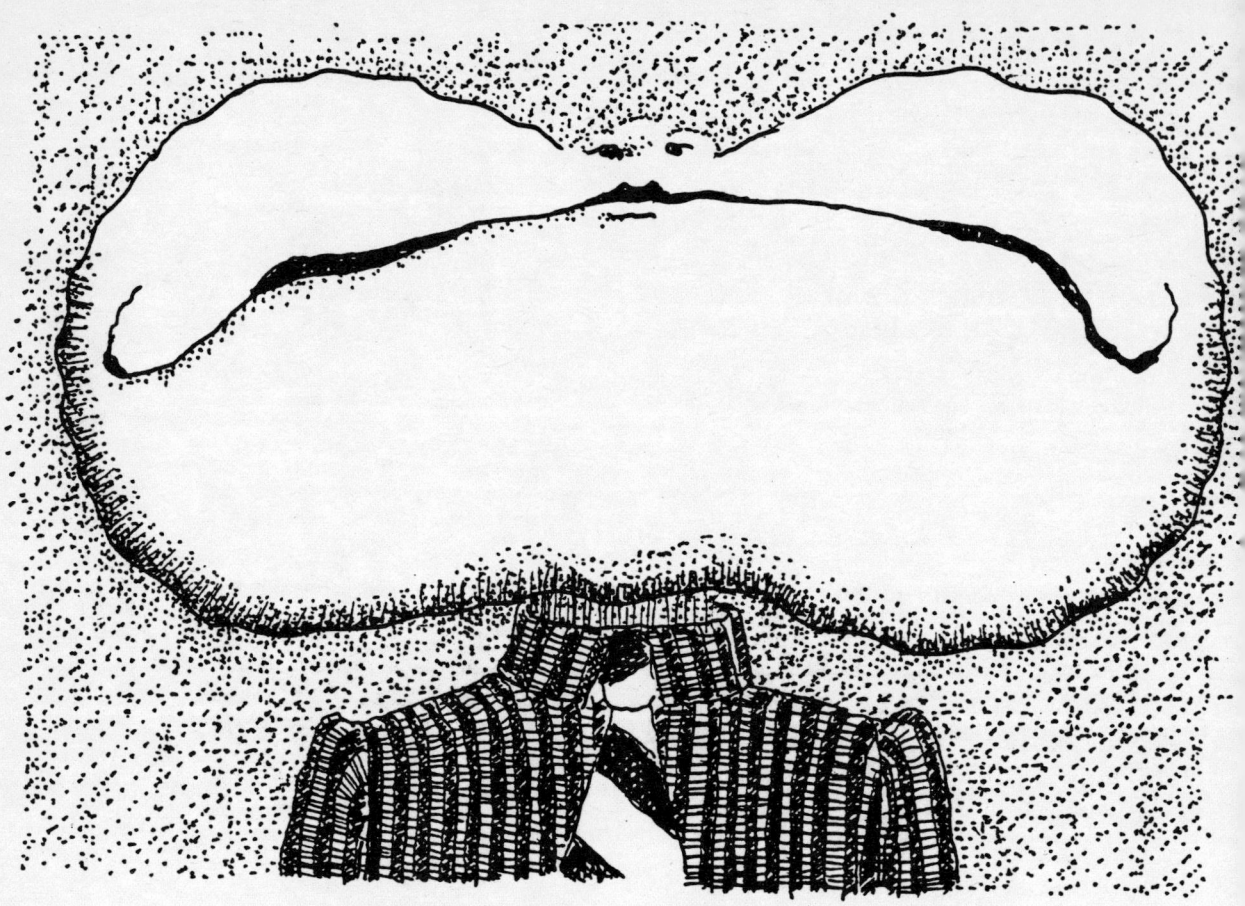

Compulsive swallowing

For information purposes only
The most extreme case of compulsive coin swallowing was recorded at Sedgefield General Hospital, County Durham, on 5 January 1958. James Gorman, 54, was admitted complaining of severe stomach cramps and after preliminary X-rays doctors decided to perform an emergency operation. What they discovered was a scrap metal dealer's paradise! 366 half-pennies, 11 pennies, 17 threepenny bits, 26 sixpences, and 4 shillings of pre-decimal coinage, together with 27 pieces of wire, totalling over 5 lb in weight.

Computer games

To raise money for the Council of Disabled People, Terry Smith of Hull, Humberside, aged 38 and himself disabled, played computer games non-stop for a total of 92 hours starting at 2 pm on Friday 23 August 1985 and finishing on Tuesday 27 August at 10 am.

Computer response

In September 1983 Bob Coleman of San Francisco, USA, received a neat computer form letter from Ronald Reagan, requesting support for the Republican Victory Fund. He gave the President his 'two cents worth' by sending a cheque for $0.02. But you can't hurt a computer's feelings! Coleman received, in short order, an eight paragraph letter (postage 20 cents) from the national committee which said that 'by sending such a generous $0.02 sponsorship, you have demonstrated your commitment, etc, etc.' This was followed by a Congressional VIP card, a signed portrait of Reagan and Vice President George Bush and a letter from Reagan himself beginning 'Dear Mr Coleman' and ending 'both Nancy & I send our very best wishes.'

Concorde – greatest number of trips

As of 10 January 1987, Fred Finn, 47, from Berkeley Heights, New Jersey, USA, had spent a total of £1,250,000 on trans-Atlantic Concorde flights. Fred has a special brass plaque on his favourite seat – 9a – and was awarded a small gold Concorde on a marble base to commemorate his 500th trip. Fred made his 650th crossing in January 1987.

Concrete slab smashing

Whether smashing concrete slabs and blocks with the head, hands or feet or having them smashed with a sledgehammer whilst positioned on delicate pieces of the anatomy, it seems the variations are endless.

Using only his head, Willie James Washington smashed a pile of 15 concrete slabs, each $1\frac{1}{4}$ in thick. The slabs were separated by pencils $\frac{1}{4}$ in thick and the total height of the 'target' was $22\frac{1}{4}$ in.

The thickest concrete slab ever smashed with a sledgehammer whilst resting on the head, is one of 3 in. The feat was performed on the head of Walter Cornelius on 20 September 1976 at the Dolphin, Peterborough, Cambridgeshire.

The greatest number of concrete paving slabs 1 in thick smashed consecutively across the stomach is 30 in 10 minutes. This feat was performed on Reg Morris at Pelsall Carnival and Fete, Pelsall, West Midlands, on 8 August 1982.

The greatest number of breeze blocks 3 in thick piled simultaneously across the stomach and smashed with a 16 lb sledgehammer is 14, performed on Justin Ho at Chelsea, London, on 22 March 1983.

The greatest number of $\frac{1}{2}$ in thick

concrete slabs smashed with the 'open hand' Karate chop is 21 (each supported by ¼ in pencils) by Dave McHale, 32, at Plymouth, Devon, on 13 May 1986.

Conkers

The only person to achieve the unique distinction of winning the world conker championships three times is 61-year-old fork-lift instructor Peter Mildane of Oundle, Northants, who on 13 October 1985 won his third title.

Container shifting

Crane driver Mick Potter won a crate of champagne for setting a new world record by moving sixty 40 ft containers in one hour at Felixstowe Docks, Suffolk, on 14 October 1986.

Cow pushing

On 29 November 1986, 20 members of Skirlaugh Young Farmers Club pushed a 250 lb fibreglass cow, mounted on wheels, a distance of 10 miles from Skirlaugh to Beverley, North Humberside, in the record time of 5 hr 10 min.

Cowpat catching

At the annual Cowpat Catching Championships at Yaxley, Cambridgeshire, on 14 September 1985, a new world record was

established by Duncan Pickering, Andrew Whitcombe and Stanley Tomalin (sponsored by Percival and Son). The team caught a total of 29 lb 6 oz of cowpat (not dried) within the permitted time of three minutes.

Crawling

Religious devotee, Jagdish Chandra, completed an 870 mile crawl from Aligarh to Jamma, India, on 9 March 1985 to appease the wrath of his favourite goddess, Mata. His journey began on 1 December 1983.

The longest crawl ever undertaken without cessation is one of 27 miles by Chris Lock at Durdham Downs, Bristol on 19 August 1984.

Crocheting

The largest article ever manufactured manually by one person is the 120 square metre woollen blanket, crocheted by Barbara Gilvey, 41, at her home in Wolverhampton, West Midlands. The blanket took six months to complete during which time Barbara worked eight hours a day, seven days a week.

Cuddling

The greatest number of cuddles collected from different people in one hour is 240 'good big hugs' by Lynne Castle (Miss Gravesham) on 9 September 1984 at Gravesend, Kent.

Cue throwing

The greatest recorded distance that a billiard cue (17½ oz) has been thrown, javelin fashion, is 116 ft 1 in by David Smith of Brentwood, Essex, at the Alternative Olympics, Hull, on 31 August 1986.

Custard pie – biggest

The biggest and heaviest custard pie ever made was one measuring 36 in in diameter and weighing 17 lb 14 oz by six pupils from Clayton Secondary Modern School, Oxford, on 14 April 1965.

Damages award – elephant

The highest compensatory damages ever paid to a circus elephant were made on 29 April 1983. The elephant was crippled in a collision with a lorry in 1979 and the court of Poona, India, decided that the lorry owner was at fault. He was ordered to pay the elephant 23,000 rupees (then about £1,700) compensation.

The highest damages awarded by any court in favour of a human being is $106,000,000 at Corpus Christi, Texas, USA, against the Ford Motor Company for faults inherent in a Ford Mustang car in which a 20-year-old man died as a result of an accident in 1974.

Debating

The longest recorded time that a debate has been continued (by 20 or more people) is 193 hr 49 min by the Oxford Union, Oxford University between 21 and 29 May 1986. The motion was 'Heineken refreshes the parts . . .'

Dinky toy jumping

The A-Team, a group of four motor cycle stunt men, laid claim to this record by successfully clearing 60 dinky toy cars laid side by side (10 ft 2 in) on a 50 cc mini cycle on 9 September 1984 at Gravesend, Kent.

Divorce

The longest period that it has taken for a divorce to become 'absolute' after the granting of a decree nisi is 21 years 1 month.

On 12 April 1984, Mrs Phyllis Jackson, 62, of Wickford, Essex, was granted an absolute divorce from her husband Herbert. The decree nisi was granted in February 1963 and it was not until Mrs Jackson applied for her old age pension in 1982 that she was informed that she was still legally married.

Driving test – most failures

The greatest number of driving test failures is attributable to Mrs Miriam Hargreaves of Wakefield, Yorkshire. After 39 failures and 213 lessons she finally triumphed on 3 August 1970.

Driving test pass – oldest

Retired Major Geoffrey Chance, a former High Sheriff of Wiltshire, became the oldest person ever to pass his driving test on 16 March 1984 when aged 90.

Driving in reverse

The longest recorded reverse drive is one of 7,180 miles for the round trip from New York to Los Angeles, USA, completed in 42 days by Charles Creighton and James Hargist. Their

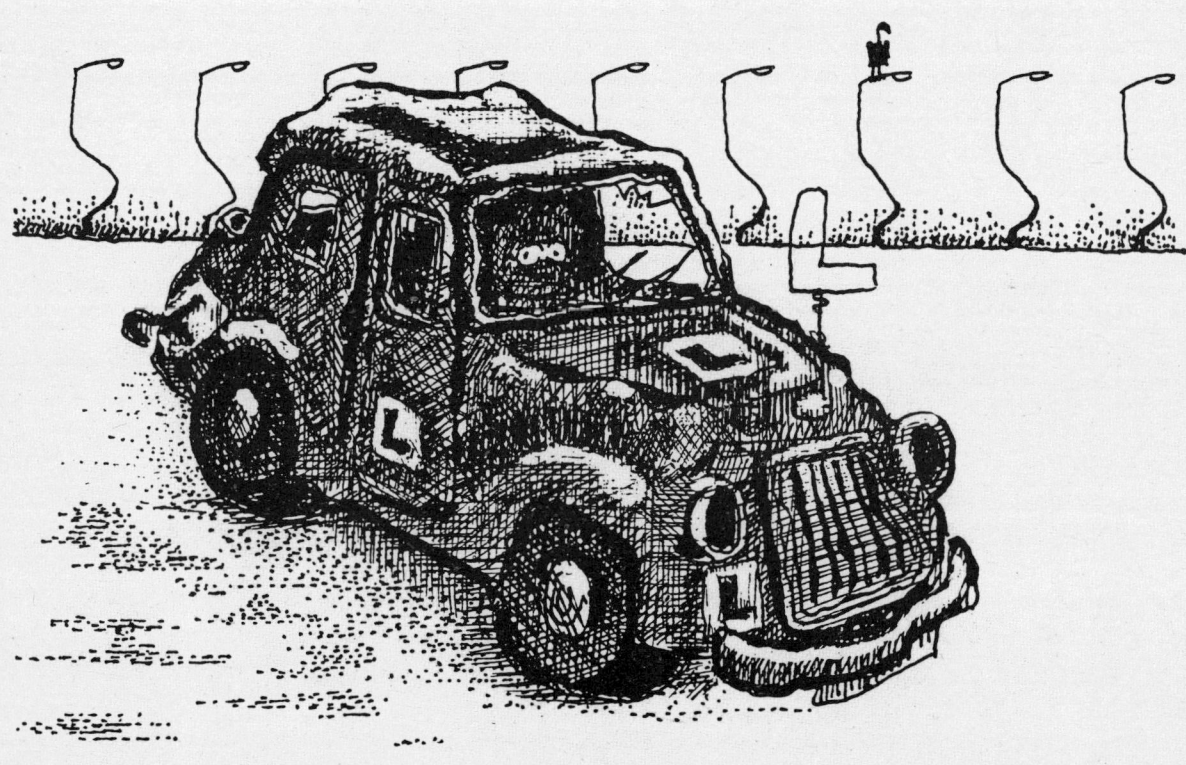

vehicle was a 1929 Ford Model A roadster which the pair had decided to test after agreeing a sponsorship deal with the Ford Motor Company. They arrived back in New York on 5 September 1930.

Drunk driving – most convictions

Irresponsible Swedish businessman Haaken Svedberg was convicted for the 58th time on 24 December 1986 of being drunk whilst driving a motor vehicle. As usual he was jailed for a month.

Duck derby

The Greater London Council's 'Thames Day' on 16 September 1984, was a 'quacking' success for the Muscular Dystrophy charity group. The world's largest no-holds-barred plastic duck race was staged with 15,000 entrants sponsored to complete the 500 yard course from Westminster Bridge to Waterloo Bridge. The fastest duck romped home in 13 minutes flat.

Egg balancing

The greatest number of fresh hen's eggs balanced in one hand is 17, by Dean Gould, 22, of Walton, Felixstowe, Suffolk, on 16 January 1987.

Egg frying

Using the same single frying pan, a team of six housewives led by Eileen Adams, 55, from Powys, Wales, set a world record at the British Gas Kitchen Centre, London, by frying 8,731 eggs in 192 hours.

Egg jumping

Tony McAbe of Manchester is the only known exponent of the art of egg jumping. So nimble and light-footed is Tony that he can jump on an egg and off again without breaking it.

Egg and spoon race

The longest distance that a fresh hen's egg has been carried in a dessert-spoon is 28½ miles by Chris Riggio of San Francisco, California, USA, on 7 October 1979 in a time of 4 hr 34 min.

Eiffel Tower

That most famous of French edifices has attracted the following record breakers.

The first (and hopefully last) man to try to fly from the Eiffel Tower was inventor Franz Reickatt. Franz had invented a special loose-fitting coat with voluminous folds of cloth which he claimed would be able to support him in such a fashion that he would glide safely to the ground. In 1912 from a platform 190 ft up the Eiffel Tower, Franz (after much hesitation) tried out his invention

and plummeted to his death. After impact his mutilated body was unceremoniously carted away by police who seemed to delight in measuring the 15 cm depression left in the hard earth.

The first people ever to parachute off the 984 ft Eiffel Tower were sweethearts Amanda Tucker and Mike McCarthy, both 23, of Yarpole, Herefordshire on 18 April 1984.

On 14 October 1905, it was reported that John Paul Cartier, 22, ran up the 729 steps of the Eiffel Tower in 3 min 12 sec.

Faggot flinging

At the re-inauguration of the once famous sport of Faggot Flinging at Brierley Hill, West Midlands, on 26 May 1984, outright victors were Pam Cook (thrower) and Steve Carrol (catcher and eater) representing The Exchange pub. In the heat of the day, the judges forgot to count how many faggots were caught and eaten – perhaps they'll let me know next year!

Fastest teddy bear

Mr Whoppit, a teddy bear owned by the late Donald Campbell, holds the world speed record for land and water. Whilst breaking and creating new land and water speed records, Donald would always be accompanied by Mr Whoppit, tucked safely under the seat. On that fatal day of 14 January 1967, Donald's turbo jet engined Bluebird K7 achieved a speed of 328 mph just prior to crashing. Very little wreckage was ever recovered and the body of Donald Campbell was never found, but floating and bobbing at the scene of the crash on Coniston Water, Cumbria, was Mr Whoppit.

Ferret legging

The undisputed world Ferret Legging Champion was 78-year-old Reg Mellor (d. 1987) of Barnsley, Yorkshire. Indeed Reg claimed to be the originator of the 'sport' when, as a boy of eight, he used to keep his hunting ferrets warm and dry by stuffing them down his trousers after a day in the fields.

On 5 July 1981, at the annual Pennine Show at Holmfirth, Yorkshire, Reg broke his own world record by keeping two live ferrets down his trousers for a time of 5 hr 26 min. Reg performed the feat in front of over 5,000 people and although badly bitten in 'all the wrong places', he persevered to the bitter end. N.B. During record attempts no undergarments can be worn, and the trouser bottoms must be firmly secured with string.

Fighting in armour

Wearing full weight (60 lb) armour and using 10 lb swords, Stephen Thomas and Khrys Yuen of the York Company of Knights performed 9½ sets (each set is six strokes) in two mins whilst fighting at Patrington Haven, Humberside, on 13 July 1986.

Fire eating

Roberto Kalin of Bregenz, Austria, set a new world record for fire eating on 29 May 1986 by extinguishing 14,648 flaming brands in two hours exactly at Ried in Austria.

Fire running

On 26 May 1985, Johnny Carr ran 220 yards along Ferensway, Hull, Humberside, with a blazing cloak strapped to his back, in 32 seconds.

Fire spitting

Joint world record holders for fire spitting are Reg Morris of Brownhills, West Midlands, and Johnny Carr of Hull, Humberside, both with a distance of 27 foot exactly.

Fistful of money

On 17 May 1985, Dennis Finney, 40, of Brading, Isle of Wight, balanced £50 worth of 50 pence pieces (100 coins) in his hand for a period of one minute.

Flapjack

The largest flapjack ever made was produced on 18 August 1984 at Swanton, Vermont, USA. A cement truck was used to mix the batter and a helicopter to do the flipping of this 20 ft diameter monster. The four inch deep flapjack contained 100 gallons of milk and 800 lb of pancake mix, took two hours to cook and could feed 15,000 people. It was topped with 1,000 lb of butter, 150 gallons of maple syrup and ¼ tonne of blueberries.

Flat cap throwing

On 17 July 1986, at Stockport, Cheshire, Tony Moxon, 30, broke his own world record for flat cap throwing by achieving a distance of 82 ft 9½ in.

Floating wheelchair

The greatest recorded distance that a floating wheelchair has been propelled over water is 24 miles, from Westminster Pier down the River Thames to Richmond. Disabled ex-soldier Charles Hankins, 64, performed this remarkable feat on 22 July 1984.

Flying bra

Human cannon ball Miss 'Rita Thunderbird', clad only in a skimpy gold lamé bikini climbed into the barrel of her cannon on 6 August 1977. And there she remained despite the successful discharge of the gunpowder propellent. Her bikini top, however, decided to do otherwise and was blasted an estimated 40 ft into the River Thames at Battersea, London.

Flying deckchair

The pilot of a reconnaissance aircraft scrambled over Los Angeles, California, USA, on 24 July 1983, in order to investigate reports of a UFO, had the shock of his life when the UFO turned out to be a UFD (Unidentified Flying Deckchair).

Madcap Larry Walters had attached 42 gas-filled weather balloons to a deckchair and had soared to the record height of 16,000 ft. Larry made a controlled descent in his 'craft' by bursting several balloons with an air pistol.

Fraud – most ambitious

Nigerian labourer Manosit Ngora received his pay cheque on 24 March 1967, a paltry nine pounds and four shillings for a month's work on a Lagos building site. Being the ambitious type, he altered the figures to read £697,000,090. 4s. Not surprisingly the cashier at his local bank refused to cash it and called the police!

Free-fall motor cyclist

On 17 August 1986, American stuntman Arnie Scholes broke the world height record for a free-fall motor cyclist. He drove his 350 cc motor cycle out of the cargo hold of a plane at 8,200 ft over the Nevada Desert. Rider and machine parachuted safely to the ground with the bike still ticking over, landed and accelerated away as Arnie detached the chute.

Fruit machine jackpot

1984 started in the best possible manner for Californian grape grower, Rocco Dinubilo. On 1 January he was presented with a cheque for $2,478,716 by the management of Harrah's Tahoe Cassino, Nevada, USA, where 24 hours earlier he had won the largest ever jackpot on a fruit machine.

General election – biggest bet

In May 1983 an anonymous punter from the Cotswolds staked £90,000 on the Conservatives to win the election. The bet was placed at Coral's in Fleet Street, London, at odds of 2–9. Directly after taking the bet, the odds were reduced to 1–6.

Grape catching

On 14 October 1979, Geoff Flounders of Salford, Manchester caught a grape in his mouth, thrown 187 ft by his brother Peter.

The greatest height from which a grape has been dropped from a moving aircraft (in this case a balloon) and caught in the mouth is 30 ft by Peter Tilney (dropper) and Tony Gough (catcher) on 25 July 1985. The pair had aimed for greater heights, but were foiled by a thick

mist rising from the river Severn at Attingham Park, Shrewsbury, Shropshire.

Reliable information has it that Paul Tavilla caught a grape in his mouth dropped 520 ft from the top of a building in Boston, Massachusetts, USA, on 9 July 1985.

The solo grape catching record belongs to Camilo Antonio Mendez of Folkestone, Kent, when on 14 January 1980, he caught a grape in his mouth, thrown a distance of 39 ft 6 in.

Grave digging

According to reliable information, Johan Thieme, sexton of Aldenburg, Germany, dug 23,311 graves during his 50 year career ending with his own burial in 1826.

Guy Fawkes

The largest guy ever built was one measuring 62 ft 4 in by the Fermain Youth Club, Macclesfield, Cheshire, on 4 November 1983.

Gym mat – most people on

At the Foster's Festival of Records, Gravesend, Kent, on 9 September 1984, 30 members of the MEPA Gym Club succeeded in piling their bodies on to a 6 ft × 4 ft padded gym mat.

Haggis hurling

The longest recorded distance for throwing a haggis is 163 ft 9½ in by Alan Pettigrew at the Ardrossan Highland Games, Scotland, on 14 June 1981.

The Scottish RSPCA are now considering a total ban on this sport as the haggis is now Scotland's rarest animal. After pleas from the World Wildlife Organisation the haggis is now listed as an endangered species.

Hair – longest

The longest hair in the world (which is still growing) belongs to 41-year-old Georgia Sebrantke of Wuppertal, West Germany. As of 28 January 1987 her tresses measured 9 ft 9 in.

The longest hair in Great Britain is worn by Dhorie Geronimo of London, the latest length of which is exactly 6 ft.

Both these ladies have a long way to go to beat the record reported in 1949 of Swami Pandarasann-adhi of Madras, India. It was claimed that he had never had a haircut in his life and that at the age of 50 it measured exactly 26 ft in length.

Hamburger heaving

Using a full-size Chinese wok (a bowl-shaped frying pan), Trevor Tass, 24, of San Francisco, USA, propelled a half-pound cooked hamburger, 'sling-shot' fashion, a distance of 80 ft on 4 July 1982.

Hand shaking

On 22 March 1985, Andrejev Wdowidowski set a new world record for hand shaking by shaking hands with 25,133 total strangers in 16 hours in the city centre of Warsaw, Poland.

Hanging

The first man ever to have survived three attempts at execution by hanging was the self-confessed murderer Joseph Samuels. He was reprieved in 1803 after the rope broke on the first and third attempts and the trap door failed to open on the second.

The only other person known to have survived three attempts was convicted murderer John Lee. On 15 November 1884 Lee was convicted of murdering his employer, Emma Ann Whitehead Keyse of Babbacombe, Devon, and sentenced to death by hanging. The attempted executions took place on 23 February 1885 at Exeter jail. In the space of seven minutes, hangman James Barry failed three times to get the trap door open and the Home Secretary, Sir William Harcourt, who was witness to the event, commuted the sentence to life imprisonment. Lee was a model prisoner, and on his release in 1917 he emigrated to the United States, married and lived a peaceful and law-abiding life until his natural death in 1933.

Hankie hurling

The hankie must be 15 inches square and weigh no more than 13.5 grammes in a dry state (not to be sneezed at!). At the annual Hankie Hurling Championships at Adastra Park, Hassocks, West Sussex, on 6 September 1986, Richard Hodgekinson of Hurstpierpoint, West Sussex, set a new world record with a distance of 185 ft 2 in.

A new female record of 111 ft 7½ in was also set by Anita Janman of Hassocks, West Sussex.

Hiccuping

Charlie Osborne of Anthon, Iowa, USA, holds the unenviable world hiccup marathon record. From 1922 to date he has hiccuped without cessation, at rates varying from 20 to 40 per minute. Doctors believe that his malady started when Charlie burst a small blood vessel

at the base of his brain when he tried to lift a huge pig at his father's farm. Charlie's total number of hiccups to date is approximately 1,009,152,000.

High altitude Morris dancer

Keith Naylor, 25, of Laughton, Yorkshire, holds the world record for the highest ever Morris dance, performed at a height of 20,000 ft above sea level. On a climbing expedition to the Himalayas, Keith took along his bells and hankies and performed his feat close to the summit of Mount Cholaste on 23 June 1983.

High kicking

The fastest recorded time for completing 50 high kicks (foot above shoulder) is 24 seconds, by Ian Fox, 21 of Crich, Derbyshire, on 1st March 1987.

Hod carrying

On 28 June 1984, at Hever Castle, Kent, Jim Ford of Bury, Lancashire, set a new world record for hod carrying. The giant hod contained 355 lb of house bricks and was carried up a 12 ft ladder at an angle of 60 degrees from the horizontal.

Hopping

Alex Smith, 18, of Corby, Northants, hopped on one leg a distance of one mile around Banbury High School playing field in the record time of 29 min 58 sec on 27 August 1972.

On 17 December 1963, Walter Cornelius set a new duration record by hopping on one leg for 1 hr 30 min at Peterborough, Cambridgeshire.

Hop scotch

The longest recorded hop scotch marathon was one of 101 hr 15 min by Mark Harrison and Tony Lunn between 30 September and 4 October 1985 at The Studio Night Club, Leicester.

Hot water bottle inflating

The fastest recorded time that a hot water bottle – manufactured to British Standard BS 1970 – has been inflated and burst (achieving a minimum circumference of 7 ft) is 1 min 30.5 sec by Fred Burton of Cheadle, Staffs on BBC's Breakfast Time on 19 October 1984.

The greatest circumference ever achieved in the inflation of a hot water bottle was 20 ft 9 in (Super Suba Seal type) by Mel Robson of Newcastle, Tyne & Wear.

House of cards

The greatest height to which a house of cards has ever been built is 12 ft 3 in by John Sain at South Bend, Indiana, USA, between 6 and 12 May 1984.

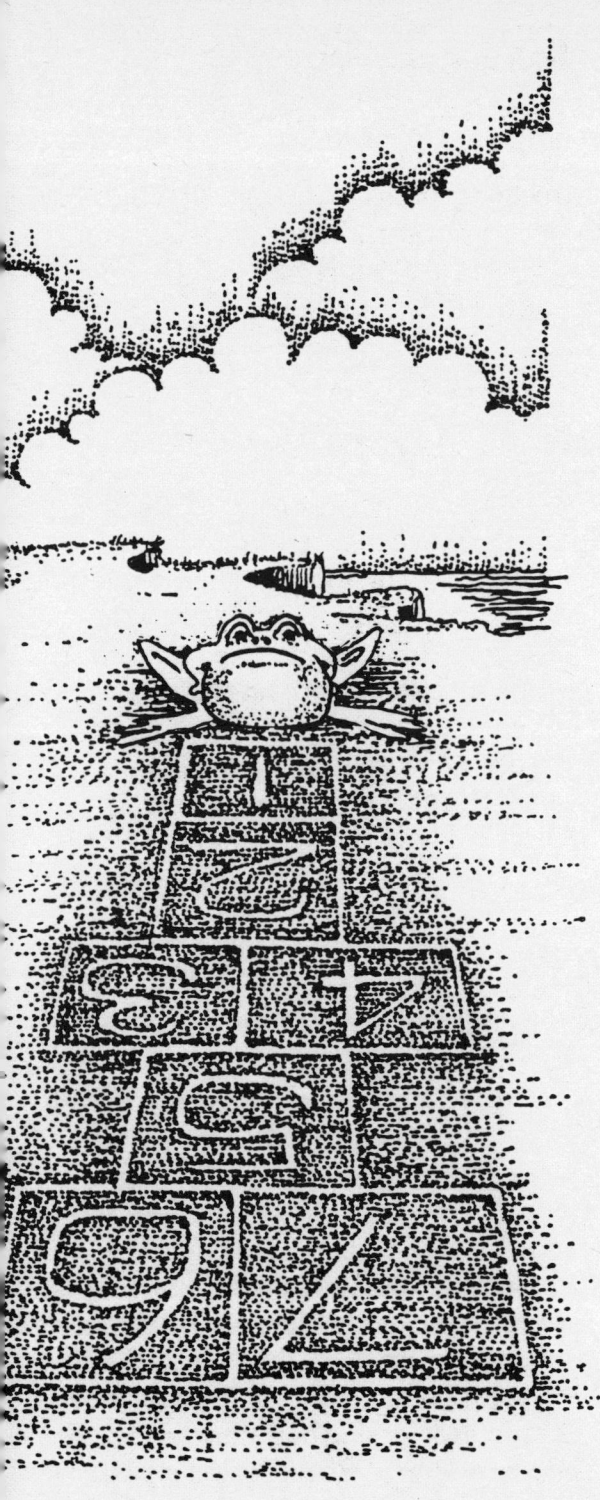

House carrying

In Canton, North Carolina, USA, they take the expression 'house moving' literally. In a race between a team of athletes and a combined team of body-builders and weight-lifters (both teams having the same total weight) each team had to lift and carry a 55 ft × 25 ft house weighing 34,000 lb. The winners were the body-builders and weight-lifters who covered the 50 yard course in 1 min 2.5 sec.

Human de-frosting device

In the winter of 1979, Peter Rowlands set a record he would probably rather forget. Finding the lock on his car frozen, he decided to breathe warm air on to it. Unfortunately his lips brushed against the lock and became stuck fast, where he remained for a painful 20 minutes before eventually freeing himself.

Hunting horn blowing

The longest recorded continuous blow on a hunting horn (using a nose-clip to prevent nasal breathing) is one of 1 min 12.1 sec by Fred Burton of Cheadle, Staffs, on 14 January 1983.

Ice bath

Under the watchful eye of a team of doctors and scientists, Edgar Rowe, 43, lay submerged up to his neck in a bath

tub full of ice water – temperature 0°C –
for the record time of 19 min 30 sec at
Cape Town, South Africa, on 3 April
1986.

Igloo marathon

Mystic Jim Randi, 46, entombed himself
unclad in an ice igloo under strict
medical surveillance, for 43 min 8 sec in
Boston, Massachusetts, USA, on 31
August 1974.

Ironing

In Melbourne, Australia, on 9 March
1973, Mrs J. Massen, 37, completed the
longest recorded ironing marathon,
89 hr 32 min.

Jet-powered truck

One of the most powerful trucks in the
world is owned by Steve Murty of
Hebden Bridge, Yorkshire. Salvaged
from an RAF Lightning fighter plane, the
engine delivers a 12,000 lb thrust and
uses 25 gallons of fuel to the mile. The
Murty Jet Truck currently holds two
European records. The standing quarter
mile was covered in 11.9 seconds with a
terminal speed of 135 mph on 24 June
1984. The outright speed record of 150
mph was achieved at Cranfield Airfield
on 21 September 1985.

Joke cracking

The longest ever joke cracking marathon
was performed by Tim Benber of
Chicago, Illinois, USA, for a 48 hour
period between 27 and 29 December
1984, at the Mount Prospect Snuggery,
Illinois, USA.

Kennel –
most expensive

German Shepherd dog 'Solar' has the
world's most expensive kennel. Features
in the 8 ft square brick-built bungalow-
type kennel include net curtains, fitted
carpets, a 4 ft square double bed with
luxury quilt, doggy ornaments on the
window sill, electric strip lighting, power
sockets for central heating and running
water. The cost to Solar's owner, Mr
Martin Pidd of Goole, Humberside, was
a mere £3,000.

Kissing – duration

On Brighton pier on 17 August 1976,
Jim Patterson and his girlfriend Toni
Smith exchanged kisses at an average of
one every 0.35 of a second. They
continued embracing each other for a
period of two hours to set a new world
record of 20,010 kisses.

It must be stressed that the kisses were
'lips to cheek' and only one of them was
pecking at a time.

The longest and probably most
meaningless kissing marathon ended on
24 September 1985 after 17 days 10

hours and 30 minutes, when Eddie Leven and Delphine Crha finally parted from their embrace to be escorted to Chicago State Hospital to receive treatment for lip blisters and sores.

Kissing – highest number

At British Telecom's Mobile Communication Carnival Day, held at Birmingham on 16 November 1985, Miss Jo Smith of Aston University set a new world record by kissing 4,726 different people in the allotted time of 8 hours.

Jo's only complaint was that she suffered a sore face, brought about by the amorous intentions of men with beards.

Kissing – underwater

It was reliably reported that on 2 April 1980 in Tokyo, Japan, Toshiaki Shirai and Yukiko Nagata remained locked in an underwater osculatory embrace for the record time of 2 min 18 sec. The British record stands at 2 min 7.6 sec, set by two young people who wish to be known only as Vicky and David, on BBC TV's 'The Late, Late, Breakfast Show' on 26 October 1985.

Lamp post – tallest

The tallest lamp posts in the world are the four installed on 17 September 1985 at Sultan Qaboos Sports Complex, Muscat, Oman. They are each 208 ft 4 in high and were manufactured by Petitjean & Co. of Troyes, France.

Land Rover – most people on

On 2 January 1986, 170 members of the Gurkha Regiment of Hong Kong piled on to a Land Rover and drove a distance of 25 metres in 50 seconds exactly.

Latrine pit digging

Mr July Nkomo of Mudiwie, Zimbabwe, bettered his own world record when, between 14 and 16 May 1986 he dug a 2 metre deep and 5 metre long latrine pit, using only a pick and shovel, in 78 hr 16 min.

Magic square

A magic square is an arrangement of numbers in the shape of a square. The numbers are arranged so that the sum of each horizontal row, each vertical column and each diagonal row are equal.

The largest magic square ever completed was by 13-year-old Wayne Tulip of Jacksonville, Florida, USA, in 1975. Each row added up to an amazing 578,865.

40

Marriage – greatest age difference

The greatest difference in age between marrying adults is 88 years in the case of Imam Ali Azam, 104, and his bride, 16-year-old Marium Begum. Ali, as his title suggests, is a priest. They were married on 22 April 1983 in the village of Fateabad, Chittagong, Bangladesh.

Unfortunately, the local villagers disapproved of the marriage because it was Ali's fifth, and under Islamic Law he was allowed only four. Ali explained that he had to marry the girl to save her from starving to death.

Matchstick model

The largest and most magnificent model ever made completely of matchsticks is a three-quarter size 1908 Rolls-Royce Silver Ghost constructed by Mr Reg Pollard of Manchester. Using only first grade matchsticks selected by his wife, Madge, from bundles of 22,000, Reg took 3,309 hours from start to finish. The total number of matches used was 1,016,711 and 63 pints of glue were needed. Placing the matches end to end would create the world's longest lucifer at 37 miles 545 yards 5 inches.

Mileage record

On 17 March 1987, it was reported that a Volkswagen 'Beetle', bought new in 1950 by Mr Tony Levy of Ickenham,

Middlesex, had clocked up a total of 798,160 miles.

Monte Carlo mint

On 18 August 1913 there was an unprecedented and as yet unequalled event at the famous casino in Monte Carlo when black came up 26 times in succession on the roulette wheel. Theoretically, a punter 'riding his luck' could have walked off with a cool one billion francs for a mere 20 franc stake.

Mop bucket carrying

The greatest number of 3 lb galvanised mop-buckets carried the statutory

distance of 50 ft is 31 by Brian Pratt of Hull at the Alternative Olympics in Hull on 31 August 1986. At the same event a new female record was set by Myra Moggridge of Steeton, West Yorkshire, with a total of 21.

Motor bike – fire leap

On 16 May 1984 at Trentham Gardens, Staffs, John 'Golly' Goddard set a new world record Fire Leap by jumping his motor bike over a mass of blazing hay, a distance of 89 ft 8 in. On landing, he parted company with his bike and skidded 50 ft through the flames. He was saved from serious injury by his special protective overalls.

Motor bike – Land's End to John O'Groats

On 2 October 1983, Tony Goulding, 35, of Retford, Nottinghamshire, set a new record by riding the 930 miles from Land's End to John O'Groats in 11 hr 58 min.

Motor car – longest distance

The longest non-stop distance ever covered by a motor car is the 7,500 mile journey from Alaska to Mexico achieved by American Louis Mattar in his Cadillac.

Specially adapted for long-distance, non-stop travel, the car features a bed, fridge, freezer, barbeque, washing machine, ironing board, bar, TV, telephone, toilet, shower, and drinking fountain. Retractable bogie wheels enable the car's wheels and tyres to be changed on the move.

On 23 February 1986, the car had covered a total of 511,200 miles on the same engine. The average fuel consumption is a mere 10 mpg which is maintained on ultra-long-distance trips by a small tanker of petrol towed behind.

Mouse catching

The most prolific Mouse Catcher of all times was 'Towser', the resident tortoiseshell cat at Glenturret Distillery, Crieff, Scotland. Born on 21 April 1963, Towser caught the grand total of 28,899 mice before her sad death on 20 March 1987. The kills were religiously recorded by Sales Manager, Peter Fairlie, who will now be searching for an adequate replacement.

Mousetrap

The fastest-acting mousetrap ever made is 'The Little Nipper', manufactured by Proctor Brothers of Bedwas, Gwent, Wales. The time from when the hungry mouse alights on the trap to when the breakback arm snaps on to its unsuspecting victim is 10.38 milliseconds (a fraction more than one hundredth of a second).

Murderess – world's most determined

In January 1978 it was reported that an unnamed 36-year-old American woman was to be tried for the murder of her husband. Before finally succeeding by dropping tranquillisers into his beer and smashing his skull with a steel weight, she first tried putting a large dose of LSD in his toast; serving him with blackberry pie containing the venom sack of a tarantula spider; placing bullets in the carburettor of his lorry; tossing a live electric wire into his shower; and injecting air into his veins with a hypodermic needle to induce a heart attack.

Musical chairs

The world's largest ever game of musical chairs, involving 5151 players, was won by Bill Bronson at the University of Notre Dame, Indiana, USA, on 6 September 1985.

Nail breaking

The fastest recorded time that a six inch nail has been broken is 5.7 seconds by Harold Cope, 50, of Derby, at Peterborough, on 28 January 1963. On the same date, Harold went on to break five six inch nails consecutively in the record time of 58 seconds.

Nail hammering and extraction

Londoner Trevor Barnett – 'The East Finchley Samson' – holds the world nail hammering record. Using only his bare hands, Trevor hammered a 12 inch nail through a six inch piece of timber in exactly 29 seconds on Yorkshire Television's 'Just Amazing' programme. The point of the nail must press at least three inches through the wood. Being a tidy soul, Trevor removes the nails with his teeth. The fastest time in which Trevor has extracted a nail in this manner is 35.2 seconds.

Names – most

A baby daughter, born to proud parents John and Margaret Nelson of Barrow Hill, Chesterfield, Derbyshire, on 31 December 1985, has been christened with 139 forenames. She will probably be known by only the first of those – Tracy.

Needle threading

An unverified report, recently received, details the ability of Dean Gould of Felixstowe, Suffolk, to thread a number 13 darning needle 3,858 times in two hours.

Newspaper boy – oldest

On 29 October 1985, 82-year-old Joe Unsworth finally hung up his paper-boy bag after a career spanning 72 years. Joe of Hindley, Lancashire, started work as a paper-boy at the age of 10 on a wage of one penny (1d) per week.

Newspaper – least successful

The least successful of any newspaper ever printed was the ill-fated *Commonwealth Sentinel*, founded in London by Lionel Burleigh. 50,000 copies were printed on the evening of 6 February 1965 and delivered to Brown's Hotel in Albemarle Street, London, where Mr Burleigh was staying with his daughter. Unfortunately they had forgotten to arrange for the paper's distribution and were ordered by police to remove the offending packages from the pavement outside the hotel. Rumour has it that Miss Burleigh managed to sell one copy to a passer-by but, by the time the newspapers were removed from outside the hotel, the news was no longer news. The *Commonwealth Sentinel* closed on 7 February 1965.

Noodle making

The fastest recorded time for making over 2,000 strings of noodles (in this case 2,048) is 34.5 seconds by Mark Pi at the China Gate Restaurant, Columbus, Ohio, USA, on 12 February 1983.

Nose poking

Darren Smith, 14, of Wolverhampton, West Midlands, set a new nose poking record on 19 February 1986 by attaining 12 hrs 30 mins with the little finger of his right hand pushed up his left nostril.

Oldest man alive

Islamic holy man, Sayed Abdul Mabood, has certified evidence (his passport) that he is over 163 years old. His date of birth is recorded as 13 December 1823 and according to officials that's no mistake! Sayed is a well-respected holy man in his local community in Pakistan and has high-ranking friends in government and religious circles. His eldest living son is 104, he is grandfather to 218 children, great-grandfather to 319 children and great-great-grandfather to 36 children.

Onion peeling

On 28 October 1980, Alfonso Salvo of York, Pennsylvania, USA, peeled 50 lb of onions (52 onions) in the record time of 5 min 23 sec.

Operations – largest number

Fifty-two-year-old Joe Ascough of Lenton Abbey, Nottingham, is the unenviable holder of the world record for having the largest number of surgical operations. At regular intervals for the past 51 years Joe has had to have operations for the removal of growths (papillomas) from his windpipe to enable him to breathe correctly. His total on 30 March 1987 is an amazing 337.

Operations – longest wait

David Carver of Torquay, Devon, claimed a new world record on 20 January 1984 following an operation for the removal of a hare-lip, after being on the National Health Service waiting list for 31 years.

Orange – oldest

The world's oldest orange is the family heirloom of Mrs Iris Lawton, 60, of Ecclesfield, Sheffield, Yorkshire. The fruit, now black and shrivelled, was given to a dying child – her husband's great uncle – 104 years ago.

Out of this world – (well, nearly)

An attempt by an American company, 'Celestis', to put the first cemetery in space has been refused planning permission by Florida's planning controller. Apparently the orbiting satellite does not provide for '. . . a paved road and chapel or optional rose garden.' Tickets for transportation to the final frontier cost $3,000 each.

Oyster opening

The greatest number of oysters opened in one hour is 1,106 by Jean-Claude Pettane at Lyons, France, on 12 December 1986.

Paella – world's largest

A ten-tonne crane was needed to lift the world's largest paella off the fire at Avilés, Spain, on 1 August 1986. The gigantic meal – enough to serve 18,000 people – was 12 metres in diameter and weighed 1,200 kgs.

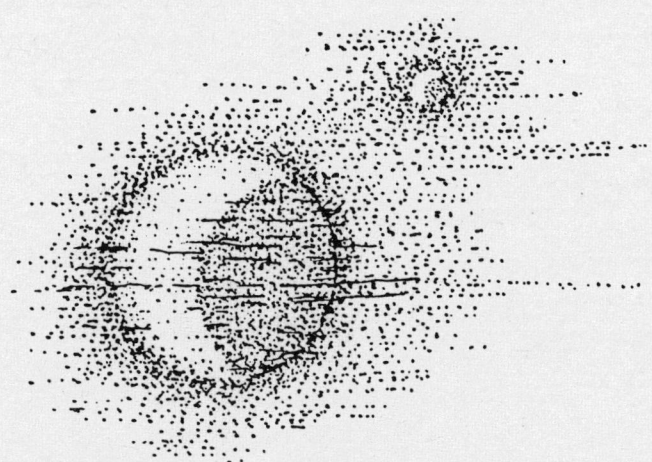

47

Pancake throwing

By using a secret thickening ingredient, David Walsh of Melbourne, Victoria, Australia, is able to produce throwable, yet edible pancakes ¼ inch thick. David projects them like frisbees. His best throw achieved a distance of 63 ft 8 in on 26 February 1986.

Pancake tossing

On 26 February (Shrove Tuesday) 1974, Mrs Sally Cutter of Limasol, Cyprus, achieved 5,010 tosses in 65 minutes, an average of one toss every 0.78 seconds.

Mary Kennedy, 22, of Aylesbury, Bucks, managed 80 tosses in one minute on Shrove Tuesday in 1976; an average of one toss every 0.75 seconds.

Paper chain (1)

By using 125,000 staples, children at Thorpe le Soken, Essex, made the world's longest paper chain of 8 miles 897 yards from 24 to 25 May 1975 – a period of exactly 24 hours.

Paper chain (2)

From correspondence received, there will be several attempts during 1988 to break the world record for the longest paper chain ever made.

The most ambitious of these attempts has already been started. Peter Stewart, 28, of Wednesfield, Wolverhampton, aims to create a paper chain 240,902 miles long!! That's 10 times the circumference of the Earth.

As a fund raising scheme for the Save the Children Fund, Peter is selling the links for 10 pence each and aims to get contributions from every school in the world. We'll keep you advised of his progress.

Paper plane

The furthest distance that a paper plane has travelled, over level ground, is 193 ft, propelled by Tony Felch at La Crosse Center, Wisconsin, USA, on 21 May 1985.

Parking tickets

The greatest recorded number of parking tickets issued by a traffic warden is 17,000 in a 15 year career by John (Bacon Face) Hancock, 57, of Old Basford, Nottingham.

Parsnip – longest

The longest parsnip ever grown is one measuring 35 inches from tip to head by Andrew Skippiness, of Ipswich, Suffolk. This was reported on 20 January 1983.

The heaviest parsnip was one weighing 10 lb 8½ oz, grown by Mr Charles Moore of Peacehaven, Sussex, in 1980.

Paydeal – longest negotiation

Negotiations lasting 40 years came to a profitable conclusion on 19 October 1983 for a group of 854 Aborigines who helped to man Australia's defences during World War II. They claimed that they should have received the same rate of pay as white troops instead of just half the rate. In conceding that the Aborigines' claim was just, the Australian Government agreed to pay out a total of £4 million in back pay to the 854 Thursday Islanders, spread over a three year period.

Pea pushing

Using only the nose and with fresh peas, the current records for pushing a pea are:

    100 yards in 4 min 30 sec by Helen McDonald of Derby, on 14 February 1970.

    1 mile in 6 hr 40 min by Helen McDonald of Derby, on 14 February 1970.

    2 miles by Helga Jansens of Peterborough, Cambridgeshire, in 15 hr 28 min on 15 August 1978.

The longest distance a pea has ever been pushed is 2 miles 50 yards by Alex Crawford, 23, on 3 September 1978, at Peterborough, Cambridgeshire, in a time of 16 hours exactly.

Penny plonking

Six children from Penrith Primary School, Cumbria, claimed a new world record for throwing pennies into a 2½ gallon plastic bucket from a distance of 10 feet. On 17 June 1979 they succeeded in collecting a record 919 pennies in 15 minutes.

Phone box cramming

Pub landlord Victor Cox claimed a new world record on 7 June 1986 by cramming 15 of his regulars into a standard British Telecom phone box at his pub in Southsea, Hants.

Piano playing balloonist

On 16 November 1983, international concert pianist John Briggs of Bingley, West Yorkshire, set a new world record for piano playing. At a height of 4,000 ft in a hot air balloon, John played merry tunes on an upright piano, thereby raising £3,500 for charity.

Piano smashing

The record for smashing an upright piano into pieces small enough to be passed through a hoop nine inches in diameter is 1 min 37 sec, achieved by six members of the Tinwald Rugby Club, Ashbourne, New Zealand, on 6 November 1977.

Piano throwing

On 10 March 1983, a team of six men from Newcastle University set a world record for piano throwing of 11 ft 6 in during their Community Action Week of fund-raising events.

The female record was set by a team of six from the University of Birmingham – Wendy Hudson, Ali Tovey, Samantha Dale, Angela Hobbs, Emmerline Foster and Jane Gibbons, with a throw of exactly three feet on 16 November 1985.

Piddling pooch

Information received from Anthony Mudge of Alby sur Chéran, France, claims a world record for his dog Dumpy. Apparently on 9 April 1986,

Dumpy cocked his leg no less than 20 times in 12 minutes. Can your dog do better?

Pig kissing

The duration for kissing a pig (minimum age one month, minimum 50 kisses per minute) is 23 min 14 sec by Sergie Kelnikof at Omsk, USSR, on 17 June 1981.

Pig riding

According to reliable information, in 1885 a Swede, Gunnar Gavelin, set a world record of 27 days for travelling the 600 miles from Stockholm, Sweden, to Moscow, USSR, on the back of a pig.

Pillar box standing

The greatest number of people to pile on to or hang from a six square feet oval-topped pillar box is 33 – all members of 'Operation Raleigh' at Bishop Burton College of Agriculture, Humberside, on 29 September 1985.

Pipe smoking

The duration record for keeping a pipe alight using only one ounce of tobacco and one initial match, is claimed by Yrjo Pentikainen of Kuopio, Finland. Yrjo's marathon lasted 4 hr 13 min 28 sec from 15 to 16 March 1968.

Plane hopping

American stuntman Jim Tyler is renowned as a pioneer of the impossible. Forever searching for new stunts, Jim performed another unique feat over the Arizona Desert on 6 June 1984. Perched in the rear seat of a Steerman bi-plane, piloted by Marshall Tulls, Jim hopped out at 10,000 ft as the plane was pitched into a controlled nose dive. He then used all his skill as a trained parachutist by free falling for one mile before manoeuvring himself into position and hopping back into the same plane.

Ploughing

The fastest recorded time for ploughing an acre of land is 11 min 21.8 sec by Robert Dee at Hodstock Priory Farm, Blyth, Notts, on 1 November 1984.

Pogo-stick

The fastest human over 100 metres on a pogo-stick is Stuart Craven of Scunthorpe, South Humberside, who recorded 42.85 seconds on 13 July 1986 at Patrington Haven, North Humberside.

Polar achievement

A joint team of six American and Canadian explorers reached the North Pole after 56 days and a 500 mile journey on 11 May 1986. They beat the previous record of 58 days set by Robert Peary in 1909 and – like Peary – used only sledges, dogs and ancient navigational equipment to chart their way across the Arctic Ice.

Pom-pom

The largest pom-pom ever made is one measuring 42½ inches in circumference by Deborah Jones of Callow, Hereford, during a three week period in 1975. Made entirely of wool the monster weighs 6 lb 1 oz.

Post box – highest

Following the renewal of an accommodating telegraph pole in Ballymacra, County Antrim, Northern Ireland, on 7 March 1979, the resident postbox was replaced by the workmen at a height of nine feet above the ground. It remained in this position for some three weeks before the mistake was rectified.

Post card – longest delivery time

On 21 October 1983, the Post Office delivered a 12th birthday postcard to Michael Wheller of St Albans, Hertfordshire. It was posted on 6 June 1942 – 41 years earlier.

Potato peeling

The longest marathon spud-bash ever completed was one lasting 50 hours by Terry Smith, 39, of Hull, Humberside, from 13 to 15 August 1985. During the record breaking marathon, Terry peeled 1,612 lb of potatoes.

Potatoes in a bucket

At Felixstowe, Suffolk, on 21 March 1987, Mark Hillman (thrower) and Dean Gould (catcher) successfully propelled 10 full size potatoes and caught them in a 2½ gallon plastic bucket over a distance of 100 ft in the record time of 37 seconds.

Pudding plonking

At 'The Alternative Olympics' on 31 August 1986 at Costello International Sports Stadium, Hull, Humberside, Dave Pummell of Brentwood, Essex, set a new pudding plonking record by propelling a 1½ lb black pudding, with the aid of a frying pan, a distance of 103 feet.

Puzzle ring

The fastest recorded time for reassembling an eight-stranded puzzle ring is 56 seconds by Billy Wood of Baildon, West Yorkshire, on 4 December 1982, at the Queen's Head, Burley-in-Wharfedale, Yorkshire.

The greatest number of strands made into a puzzle ring is 24, owned by Muhamed Majerki of King Said Port, Saudi Arabia.

Queueing

Kevin Mellish, 38, of Kidbrooke, South London, holds the world record for queueing. From 7 December to 27 December 1986, Kevin queued outside the London store of Selfridges for 480 hours to buy a £700 carpet marked down to £95 in the sales.

Raffle prize

The most valuable prize ever offered for a raffle was the 390 acre estate of Mullingar, Eire, worth £1,575,000. Raffle organiser, estate owner and professional gambler Barney Curley, 44, sold 9,000 tickets at £175 each. The owner of the winning ticket was Mr Tony Ray of Tewkesbury, Gloucestershire, who shared his prize with five friends when the draw took place on 9 February 1984.

Reptile and amphibian smuggling

On 31 October 1986, Peter Loughlin, 19, and Stanley Mark, 20, both of Notting Hill, London, were found guilty of the largest ever attempt to smuggle reptiles and amphibians. They were caught by customs officers at Gatwick Airport with 246 frogs, 25 snakes and 18 terrapins crammed into their suitcases after a flight from Corfu.

Round Britain drive

On 5 October 1984, three anonymous CB radio fans completed the 3,650-mile round Britain drive in 64 hr 39 min. The three were helped by regional 'Good Buddies' giving regular 'smokie' reports.

Rubik's Cube

Vietnamese refugee, Minh Thai, 16, holds the world record for the fastest solution of the dreaded Rubik's Cube. At the World Rubik Cube Championships held in Budapest, Hungary, on 5 June 1982, Minh (then at High School in Los Angeles, California, USA) registered a time of 22.95 seconds.

In the intellectual quest for what became known as 'God's logarithm' – the fewest number of moves needed in theory to unscramble a cube – the lowest calculation was 22, but the best ever achieved was 52, by a British mathematician called Morwen B. Thistlewaite.

Rubik's Magic

Successor to the infamous cube, Rubik's Magic has 50 quintillion – 50,000,000,000,000,000,000 – ways of doing it wrong. There is only one solution! The fastest recorded time that a solution has been achieved is 11 min 14 sec, by Jonathan Pearce at Hamley's Toy Shop, London, on 17 December 1986.

Sandcastle

The world's largest sandcastle was completed in August 1986 in Florida, USA. 200 volunteers built a 13 metre high, 40 metre long, 30 metre wide replica of Bluebeard's castle. They used 3,600 tonnes of sand and 2,500 tonnes of water.

Sausage making

The world's largest and heaviest sausage was made in Geelong, Victoria, Australia, by Ian Zulic of Hero's Smallgoods on 3 November 1985. Weighing in at 3.33 tonnes, the sausage was 6.83 miles long and took 14 hours to complete.

Dave Kersey of Grimsby, South Humberside, has laid claim to the title of world champion sausage maker. From July 1975 to March 1987 Dave has regularly turned out 30,000 sausages every week, weighing almost 2 tonnes in total. The composite total of sausages made to 24 March 1987 is 18,720,000.

Scarecrow

The tallest scarecrow ever built was one constructed by members of 'Operation Raleigh' and displayed at Bishop Burton College of Agriculture, Humberside, on 29 September 1985. It measured 43 feet in height, with an arm span of 15 feet.

Settee – largest

The largest settee ever manufactured was completed in August 1984 by the Leather Suite Centre at Bamber Bridge, Lancashire. Manufactured from pink cowhide with grey trimmings it has 14 casters and 990 leather buttons sewn in – Chesterfield style. It was sold at an auction on 4 October 1984 to The Barton Grange Hotel, Preston, Lancashire, for £3,250.

Shaving

On 28 April 1983 at Gillingham, Kent, demon barber Jerry Harley shaved 987 volunteers in 60 minutes, using a safety razor. A second record went to Jerry Harley on 9 September 1984 at Gravesend, Kent, when he shaved 614 customers in one hour, using a set of well-sharpened cut-throat razors. Jerry uses the well-practised 'three-slash' technique, taking a little under six seconds to complete each shave.

Sheep to cloth

Ninety members of staff at Charles, Early & Marriot Ltd of Witney, Oxfordshire, produced fifty full-sized blankets from fleece to finished dyed article in 14 hr 4 min on 17 May 1959. It took just 8 hr 11 min to complete the first blanket.

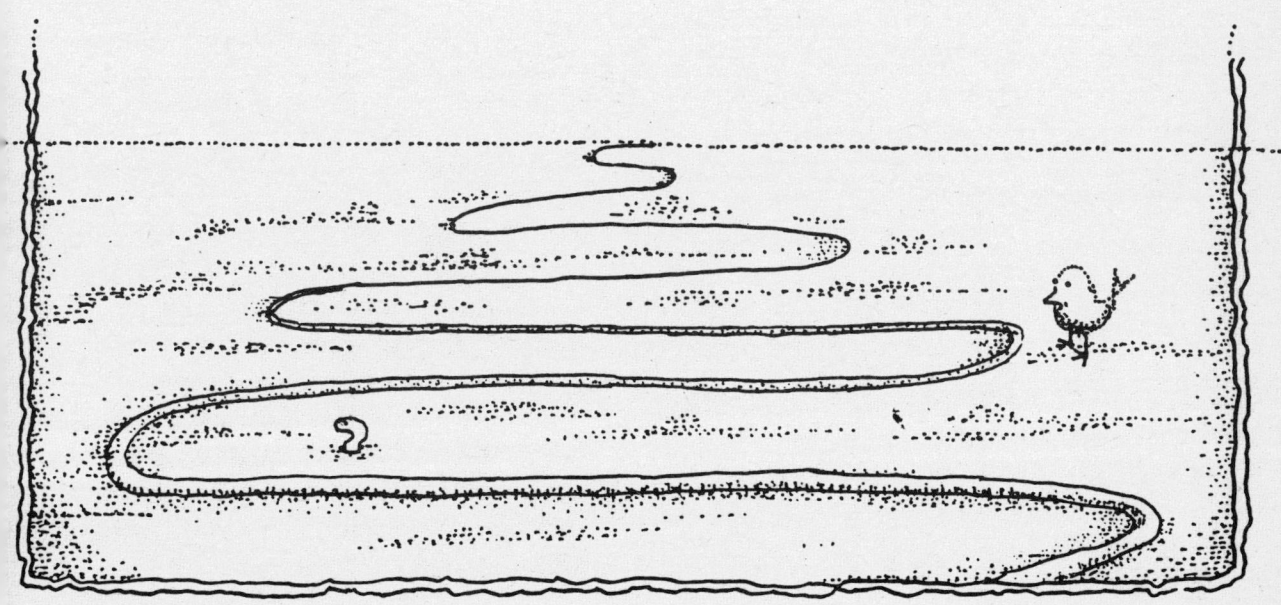

The shortest recorded time taken to transform the fleeces of three sheep into a suit of clothes has been achieved by a team of 65 members from Melbourne College of Textiles, in Australia, in 1 hr 34 min.

Sheep in a snowdrift

An overweight sheep (now nicknamed Snowdrift) survived a record 45 days trapped in a snow hole at her owner Dugald Wyper's farm at Cushnie, Aberdeenshire, Scotland. Still fit, but much slimmer, Snowdrift was dug out on 8 March 1984 after the snow had melted sufficiently (from its original depth of 10 feet) to expose her ears.

Shouting

At Parrock Street Car Park, Gravesend, Kent, on 9 September 1984, John Hughes of the Isle of Grain, Kent, set a new world record for the loudest shout ever recorded at 115.8 dBA. The shouted word must be 'Sooeee' – a recognised way of calling home pigs in the Southern States of America.

Slate smashing

Policeman Ian Womersley, 24, of Hemsworth, Yorkshire, set a new world record on 26 September 1983 by consecutively smashing 403 slates with his bare feet in 38.3 seconds.

Smoking

Ahmed Bey Zog I, King of the Albanians 1928–1946, holds the world record for the largest number of cigarettes smoked in a day. During the early part of the Nazi uprising he regularly smoked 240 cigarettes a day and even had a special stamp issued to commemorate the fact.

Frenchman John Paul Didez smoked 100 Marlboro cigarettes in 2 hr 49 min in Paris, France, on 1 October 1985.

Snake sacking

In Bolivar, Pennsylvania, USA, they practise the way-out sport of snake sacking. Five rattlesnakes are tipped from a sack at the feet of the participant who then, with ungloved hands, has to grab the snakes and stuff them, head first, back into the sack, which is held open by a colleague. The holder of the world snake sacking record is Steve Eckenroad, with a time of 5.5 seconds.

Being bitten means disqualification.

Sneezing

The most protracted bout of sneezing ever recorded is that of Donna Griffiths of Pershore, Herefordshire. Donna began sneezing incessantly on 13 January 1981 and only after special treatment at a Swiss clinic was the fit alleviated on 16 September 1983; a period of 978 days, during which she sneezed an estimated three and a half million times.

Snoring

The loudest snore in the world is the one endured night after night by Mrs Julie Switzer of Calmore, Hampshire. Husband Mel is the culprit. On 28 June 1984, at Hever Castle, Kent, Mel recorded his loudest ever snore, with an ear-shattering 87.5 decibels.

Snowman

The largest snowman ever built was by 8 members of Ski Supertravel at Val-D'Isére, France, between 21 and 24 January 1986. It measured exactly seven metres in height and had an estimated weight of 15 tonnes.

Snuff taking

In becoming National Snuff Taking Champion for the second time, 65-year-old Gerry Anderson set a new world record by sniffing 50 different samples in the alloted five minutes, at Tiverton, Devon, on 28 April 1986.

Space hopping

The fastest recorded time to cover 100 metres on a space hopper is 28.5 seconds by 11-year-old Tony Smythe of Stetchford, Birmingham, at the Birmingham Students' Carnival on 16 November 1985.

The greatest height ever cleared on a space hopper is one of 30 inches by Janina Pulaski on BBC TV on 26 May 1975.

A new space hopper long jump record of 6 ft 6 in was claimed on 7 July 1984 by 12-year-old Raymond Tulloch of Hastings, Kent.

Space invaders

Schoolboy Kaff Jackson, 15, from Exmouth, Devon, laid claim to a world record space invaders' score on 7 October 1984, when after an eight hour session his unbeaten score totalled 41,000,000.

Spitting

Wally Adams is to spitting what Barry McGuigan is to boxing – the best.

Undefeated in National Contests since 1981, Wally holds the following spitting records:

EUROPEAN RECORD
Melon Seed: 46 ft 8½ in
Cherry Stone: 48 ft 4½ in

WORLD RECORD
Grape Stone: 22 ft 4 in
Peach Stone: 16 ft 2½ in
Salted Peanut: 27 ft 11 in

On 21 February 1986, at the Fruit Market, Hull, Humberside, Wally created a new world record for spitting a coconut by achieving 9 ft 7½ in.

Spoon-hanging

Spoon-hanging is the art of balancing the bowl of a spoon on the end of the nose, with the handle hanging down towards the chin.

Keeping her head at an angle of 90 degrees to her body and using a standard teaspoon, Ami Barwell, aged seven, of Hedon, North Humberside, 'spoon-hung' for 2 hr 15 min 40 sec continuously on 10 March 1985.

Suicide – world's most unsuccessful

Hans Klaus, 43, from Kiel, West Germany, must surely hold the world record for the largest number of unsuccessful suicide attempts. Klaus tried 28 times to kill himself. His vain attempts included these methods:

Ten times he slashed his wrists; four times he took poison; twice he tried to hang himself. He also tried stabbing, gas, drowning, an overdose of drugs and falling under a car. On his final attempt on finding his wife, Eva, in bed with her lover, he dragged her from the bed and jumped backwards with her out of the fourth floor bedroom window.

She died, but Klaus landed on top of her and walked away with only minor injuries. He is now serving a jail sentence for manslaughter.

Sunflower

The tallest sunflower on record is one grown by Peter Crone of East London, South Africa, measuring 24 ft 9¼ in on 14 March 1984. The greatest number of flower heads to bloom simultaneously on a sunflower is 60, produced by a 9 ft 6 in specimen grown by Mrs Lily Chinery of Elvedon, Lancashire, during the summer of 1983.

Survival on an oxygen bottle

During normal fire fighting practice a standard (1,800 litres charges to 3,000 psi) Fire Brigade oxygen cylinder will last approximately 30 minutes.

On 9 September 1984 at Gravesend, Kent, Dick Mason breathed continuously from a single oxygen bottle for the record time of 3 hr 55 min 59 sec.

Table – most people on

In the summer of 1983 a team of gymnasts from Arizona State University, headed by coach Don Robinson, succeeded in cramming 25 people on top of a table measuring just 5 ft × 3 ft. Just for fun each gymnast had to mount the table by doing a forward somersault.

Talking – fastest

American John Moschitta was recorded as having spoken 546 words (reading from Shakespeare's *Macbeth*) in 60 seconds on Yorkshire Television's 'Just Amazing' programme on 22 April 1984.

Another accolade for Yorkshire Television is claimed by their sports commentator, John Helm, who has recited the names of all 92 clubs in the English Football League in exactly 26 seconds.

Talking – non-stop

The most protracted feat of non-stop talking was by Mr E Jayaraman, 54, of Calcutta, India, who spoke continuously for 165 hours ending on 14 September 1986.

Tattooing

At the Clifton Tattoo Studios, Northampton, on 2 July 1985, proprietor Tony Clifton completed 120 individual tattoos in one hour. The world's most tattooed lady is Rusty Field of Aldershot, Hampshire, whose body is almost 85 per cent covered.

Tea making

On 28 September 1983, 8-year-old Cub Scout Tony Murray of Barrow-in-Furness, Cumbria, completed a 14-day tea making marathon. Tony made a record 2,713 cups of tea in his allotted time.

Teeth cleaning

Pauline Mortimer, aged 14, set a new world teeth cleaning marathon record on 22 August 1981 when she cleaned her teeth continuously for 8 hr 30 min at her home in Dublin, Eire.

Telephone directory tearing

The fastest recorded time measured to tear in half 10 telephone directories (minimum thickness 2 cm) is 33 seconds by Dr Peter Altman of Edgware, Middlesex.

The greatest number of telephone directories ripped in half (minimum thickness 2 cm each) in one minute is 18, by Reg Morris of Walsall at Walsall Wood Labour Club on 14 August 1978.

Tortoise

Mrs Chris Hall of Minster, Isle of Sheppey, claims a world record on behalf of her pet tortoises Kizzy and Hercules. Over a four week period ending on 6 February 1984, Kizzy successfully hatched out 15 babies including one set of twins.

Two tortoises, Gertrude and Fred, who have been with the same Lowestoft family for over 77 years, became the oldest ever parents on 10 March 1984, when six of Gertrude's eggs hatched from the batch of eight she laid.

On 26 May 1966, *The Times* reported the death of 'Tu Malilia', the Royal Tongan Tortoise, aged 205. The tortoise was presented to the King of Tonga in 1773, when its reputed age was only 12 years, by Captain James Cook.

Tow – marine

The longest and most enterprising tow in the history of merchant shipping was the regular towing of the six-masted schooner tanker 'Navaho' (9,250 dwt – dead weight tonnage) by the steamer tanker 'Iroquois' (8,888 dwt). Built in 1907 and owned by the Anglo-American Oil Company, these two ships had a total towing partnership of more than 22 years. They traded mainly between Baton Rouge, Louisiana, USA, and Thames Haven, England: a one-way crossing of 4,930 miles. Their speed averaged around eight and a half knots and they were expected to complete some eight voyages a year. The total recorded mileage was set at 1,044,161 nautical miles – and during this time the towing hawser parted only once.

Tow – motor car

The longest recorded motor car tow in history ended on 15 October 1927. It took 89 days for Frank J. Elliott and George A. Scott to persuade a total of 168 passing motorists to tow their engineless Model T Ford the distance of 4,759 miles from Halifax, Nova Scotia, to Canada's Pacific Coast. And all for a one thousand dollar bet!

Tractor

The fastest and most powerful tractor in the world is owned by Dave Prince of Rodney Stoke, Wells, Somerset. The engine is a Rolls-Royce Merlin capable of producing 1,000 brake horse-power and was formerly fitted to a Centurian Tank. Dave's fastest attained speed to date is 130 mph achieved on 14 November 1985.

Train travel

Dave Wakefield of Walthamstow, London, claims the record for the highest mileage covered on British Rail in 24 hours. On 10 May 1986, he covered 1,622 miles.

Trapped in a whale

Apart from the Biblical story, there has indeed been a modern day Jonah. On 7 February 1891, two crew members of the American whaler 'Star of the East' were lost overboard from a small boat whilst trying to harpoon a large thrashing sperm whale. The whale was eventually harpooned and killed and winched to the deck where the wicked flensing knives soon got to work. Early on the morning of 8 February – some 16 hours later – the whale's stomach was split open to reveal the contents. Inside, unconscious but miraculously alive, with his hair and skin bleached snowy white by the whale's digestive fluids, was seaman James Bartley.

Trolley pushing

The longest recorded distance covered in 24 hours is 53 miles, completed on 18 July 1977 by Dave Patterson, 19, and Dave Brown, 20. The two Daves pushed their 'borrowed' supermarket trolley between Barnstaple, Devon, and Taunton, Somerset: whilst one was pushing, the other sat in the trolley.

Trolley standing

The greatest number of people to stand upright and unsupported in the basket of a standard supermarket trolley for a period of not less than 30 seconds is eight – members of The Princess Royal Hospital Team, Hull, at Patrington Haven, Humberside, on 13 July 1986.

The record for the greatest number of people to pile in and on a specially strengthened supermarket trolley is 29, by regulars of the Red Lion, Harlington, at the BBC TV Centre, London, on 22 February 1986.

Truck carrying

Arnie Scoles and Dick Reed of the Power Source Health Club, Los Angeles, USA, hold the world record for truck carrying with a time of 55.5 seconds. The pick-up truck must weigh 2,870 lb and the rear wheels must be lifted off the ground. The truck is then pushed along a 40 yard course.

Truck pulling

On 29 September 1985 the combined tug o' war teams (eight each) from The Shakespeare Inn and 'Terry Miller Homes' pulled a fully loaded 38 tonne truck and trailer a distance of one mile from the BP Terminal to Saltend, Humberside, in the record time of 26 min 45 sec.

Olympic shot-putter and former 'World's Strongest Man', Geoff Capes, broke his own world record for solo truck pulling at Dover, Kent, on 18 September 1986. Geoff dragged the 12½ tonne truck the required distance of 25 metres in 42.31 seconds.

Turkey – most expensive

The highest price ever paid for a turkey is £3,500 for a 77 lb 6 oz specimen auctioned at the Butchers Hall, London, on 9 December 1985. The turkey, reared in Cheshire, was later donated to local children's homes.

Two-wheel drive

Driving an Iveco 190 Tractor unit (normally used for towing 40 ft trailers), French stunt driver Gilbert Bataille performed a record breaking 60 second run on only two wheels, covering a distance of 3.80 km at Amiens, France, on 6 October 1984.

The longest recorded distance for driving on two wheels is 130 miles by Michel Signoret driving an Opel Cadet at the Paul Ricard circuit at Provence, France, on 14 March 1985.

The fastest speed ever attained driving on two wheels is 76 mph by Ken Erikson at the Anderstorp track, Sweden, driving an Opel Cadet on 28 September 1985.

Two-wheel perching

At Santa Pod Raceway on 21 August 1984, 10 members of the Steve Street Stunt Team piled into a Bedford CF 250 van. When he reached 30 mph, driver Steve Street flipped the van on to two wheels and the other nine members climbed out of the van's passenger side window to perch precariously on the sharply angled roof, so setting a new world record for two-wheeled perching.

Typing

Probably the most arduous and protracted record breaking attempt of all times is being made by Les Stewart of Mudjimba, Queensland, Australia. Forced into early retirement from the

Queensland Police Force because of a debilitating illness and 75% third-degree burns to his body, Les determined to keep himself occupied by embarking on a typing marathon using a manual typewriter.

His aim is to type all the numbers from one to one million in words. Les started his marathon in April 1982, and by 16 February 1987 he had reached 467,000. Nine thousand two hundred and thirty sheets of quarto size paper have been used and Les reckons he is well on target for the completion date – sometime in 1992!

Tyre rolling

On 17 June 1975, Walter Cornelius of Peterborough lashed together two five feet diameter tractor tyres and walked on top of them covering a distance of 25 miles in the time of 23 hr 10 min.

Tyre tossing

On 31 August 1986, Julian Stephens of Hull set a new world record for tyre tossing (170 × 14 Cortina type) at 'The Alternative Olympics', Hull, with a throw of 13.29 metres.

Underwater knitting

The longest underwater knitting marathon was one lasting just 30 minutes as housewife Janet Stevens, 38, of Netheravon, Wiltshire, sat fully submerged wearing an aqua-lung. Janet performed her feat on 30 October 1984 and successfully completed the finished article – a hot water bottle cover.

Vasectomies

The largest number of vasectomies undertaken at the same time for a specific cause took place on 8 March 1985. To celebrate the 57th birthday of King Bhumibol of Thailand, 1,200 loyal subjects were vasectomised by a team of 60 doctors who performed the operations at the rate of two every minute. All Thais vasectomised on 8 March are operated on free of charge!

Water baling

This record is for the quickest time taken to bale a 'pond-sized' amount of water out of a single receptacle. The volume is now set at 170 imperial gallons and the baling record using a No 1 size thimble is held by 12 children of the Chesterfield Young Oxfam Group, who on 15 March 1975 completed their task in 12 hours exactly.

Water-filled wellie wanging

Always a popular and entertaining feature of holiday camp fun and games, water-filled wellie wanging has now become established as a regular world championship event. Competitors must be seated in a chair or stool and throw the size 10 wellie full of water backwards over the head. The distance is measured to the first contact point with the ground.

At the first Annual Water-Filled Wellie Wanging Championships at The Black Horse Inn, Roos, Humberside, on 25 January 1986, a world record throw of 15.42 m was achieved by Mel Brewer, 27, of Bradford, West Yorkshire. At the same event a new female record was set at 7.62 m by Jean Bramhall, 25, of Bradford, West Yorkshire.

Weather balloon inflating

The shortest time taken to inflate a weather balloon up to eight feet diameter using only lung power is 57 min 7 sec by Nick Mason of Manchester in Tokyo, Japan, on 9 March 1986.

The shortest time taken to inflate two 1,000 gramme weather balloons consecutively to eight feet diameters using only lung power is 4 hr 42 min 23 sec by Fred Burton of Cheadle, Staffs, on 13 June 1982. The largest diameter to which a 1,000 gramme weather balloon has been inflated is 10 ft 8 in in a time of 5 hr 15 min by Fred Burton, at the Cheadle Festival, Staffs, on 16 July 1982.

Weddings

The record for the most weddings in a lifetime is held by King Mogut of Siam (of *The King and I* fame), who during his reign had 9,016 wives, all married individually.

Wedding train

When Karl-Heinz Woike and his bride Andrea Thyssen were married in Hamburg on 8 March 1986, more than 600 children from local youth clubs were left outside the church. They were all needed to support Andrea's wedding train – an incredible 3,000 ft of it – which encircled the local shopping centre.

Weight gain

The heaviest human in medical history was John Minnoch of Seattle, Washington, USA, whose weight in March 1978 was stated by doctors at the University Hospital, Seattle, to be 100 stone 10 lb. It was reported in October 1981 that after coming off a strict diet he gained 14 stone in 7 days.

Wellie wanging

Originated by the Druid Priests of Wetwang, Yorkshire, 'wellie wanging' is still practised today. Under modern rules the wellie must be a Dunlop Challenger size 8 and the current world record holder is Tony Rodgers of Warminster, Wiltshire, with a throw of 173 ft performed on 9 September 1978.

Two new junior (under 12) records were set on 21 May 1986 at Hoyland Springwood School, Yorkshire.
Boys: David Lewis, 11 – 83 ft 2 in
Girls: Melanie Wright, 11 – 65 ft 7 in

Wet nappy throwing

The longest recorded distance that a wet nappy has been thrown is 163 ft by Gordon Small at Graylingwell Hospital fête, Chichester, Sussex, on 29 June 1986. It is not known what mode of soiling or saturation was used!

Wheelbarrow push

The longest marathon wheelbarrow push ever recorded was one lasting 50 days and covering exactly 1,400 miles from London to John O'Groats and back by Lenny Denton, 47, ending on 20 July 1986.

Wheelchair marathon

The longest recorded distance ever travelled non-stop by wheelchair is 100 miles. The record breakers are Andy Stoner, 21, of Perranporth, and Alan Wyle, 19, of Exeter, who reached St Austell, Cornwall, on 17 April 1983. Both men are physically disabled and raised £2,500 for charity.

Wheel changing

The fastest recorded time for changing all four wheels (four stud) on a family saloon car using only manual tools is 2 min 30 sec by a team of four from Industrial Tyre Specialists, Hull, at Patrington Haven, Humberside, on 13 July 1986.

Whip cracking

In order to crack a whip, the tip must be made to travel faster than the speed of sound (1,000 ft per second). The only man ever to crack a whip over 100 ft long is Australian Noel Harris. His record breaking whip measured 105 ft 4 in and took the hides of three cows to make.

Whistling

The loudest recorded level at which a human being has whistled is 122.5 decibels by Roy Lomas at BBC TV Studios, Manchester, on 19 December 1983.

The longest recorded non-stop whistling marathon was performed by David Frank of Toronto, Canada. Between 23 and 24 November 1985, he completed 30 hours 10 minutes at The Annapurna Restaurant, Toronto, Canada.

Wicker basket

The world's largest wicker basket stands at 18 ft high and 14 ft across. Made in Germany in 1982 as a receptacle and display piece for cushions, it took 11 miles of wicker and osier to complete.

Winkle picking

The fastest recorded time for picking 50 winkles (with a straight pin) is 2 min 14.77 sec set on 25 January 1986 by Colin Ribee at the Black Horse Inn, Roos, Humberside.

Woggle hopping

The art of Woggle Hopping – vaulting over pillar boxes – originated in South Yorkshire in the 1940s and is still a popular pastime to this very day. The greatest number of woggle hops performed in one hour is 138 by David Ackroyd, 22, of Chesterfield, on 16 November 1962.

Worm charming

At the annual World Worm Charming Championship held at Willaston School, Nantwich, Cheshire, on 19 July 1980, Tom Shufflebottom set a new world record by successfully charming 511 worms to the surface in the allotted 30 minutes. Entrants are given a plot of land three metres square and one is then required to 'insert an ordinary kitchen fork into the soil and vibrate it manually.'

Worm stuffing

The world record for worm stuffing – the British Equivalent of 'Snake Sacking' – is 8.96 seconds for five worms by Helen Turner of Bedford on 16 January 1987.

'Y-front' leaping

The greatest number of times a pair of 'Y-fronts' have been donned and removed (after being pulled above the knee) in one minute is 32, by Stuart Cook of Chesham, Bucks, at 'The Alternative Olympics', Hull, on 31 August 1986.

The female record is 24, by Julie Davidson of Anlaby, Humberside, who performed the feat for Japanese Fuji Television on 31 January 1987.

Zip fastener

The longest zip fastener ever manufactured was completed on 22 January 1985 by the Italian firm of RIRI for use by Messrs Cable and Wireless in the protection of submerged telecommunication cables. At a length of 632.5 metres it has over 119,000 nylon teeth.

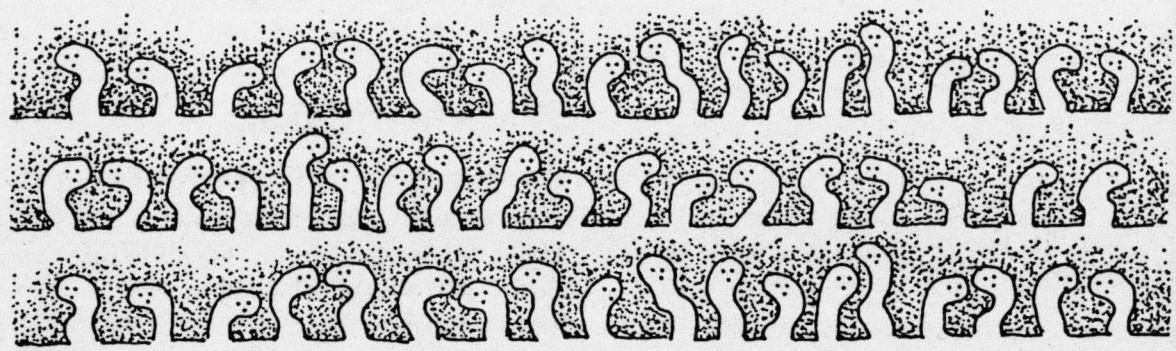

Chapter Two

COLLECTING

The Alternative Book of Records is now a record breaker in its own right, for bringing together the most bizarre and outrageous collection of people ever to have been recorded in the annals of history!

Most collectors restrict their interests to stamps, coins, football programmes, etc, but not the Alternative Record Breakers featured here. I'm sure there must be vast collections all over the world that are worthy of a mention. Does your collection of odd things qualify? Let me know.

And another thing! Is there a collective name for all these categories? I'm sure there must be. If you know, or think you know, or maybe you could make up a collective noun, let me in on the secret, care of Grafton Books.

Autographed photographs

The largest collection of autographed photographs, signed by recognised celebrities, is one of 1,782 amassed by Peter Clark of London. Peter's collection contains several unique shots of man's first moon landing in 1969, all signed by the Apollo XI astronauts.

The most expensive autographed photograph ever to change hands was of famous American gangster, Al Capone. It was bought at Hamilton Sales Galleries, New York, USA, by Barry Hoffman, for a price of $4,250 on 12 August 1982.

Bakelite

The Bakelite Museum Society was set up by Patrick Cook and now boasts about 150 members from all parts of Britain and all walks of life. Their privately owned museum in Mundania Court, Forest Hill, South London, houses Britain's largest collection of plastics and bakelite, with a total of 7,100 different items.

Barbed wire

Anthony J. Spellman of Phoenix, Arizona, USA, claims to have the world's largest collection of different types of barbed wire. One of his rooms houses 64 different types.

Beatles' memorabilia

Apart from the local council's Beatles' exhibits in Liverpool, the world's largest collector of Beatles' memorabilia is Geoff Augsberger of Normal, Illinois, USA. Latest information available has it that Geoff's collection exceeds 18,400 different items, including jigsaws, bedspreads, calendars, aprons, books and, oh yes! – records.

Beds

King Louis XIV of France had the largest collection of beds. 413 of them, all elaborately carved and gilded, were dotted about his kingdom so that wherever he travelled he could always sleep in his own bed.

Beer can ring pulls

Latest information (21 January 1987) records that the world's largest collection of beer can ring-pulls is one gathered since the Fourth of July celebrations of 1969 by the abstemious Arthur J. Jordan of Yorkstown, Virginia, USA. Arthur estimates the number conservatively at 714,100. Linked 'loop to curl' the ring-pulls would stretch to about 12½ miles in length.

Beer labels

The largest reported collection of all British beer labels is one of 29,000 collected by Keith Osborne of London. Beer label collectors are called labologists.

Beer mats

In May 1986 it was reported that the world's largest collection of beer mats, owned by Leo Pisker of Vienna, Austria, had grown to 114,960 – all different and from more than 150 countries. Beer mat collectors are called tegestologists.

Blowlamps

The largest known collection of working blowlamps is housed in The Crown Inn, Addingham, Yorkshire. As of 6 April 1987 the total was 64, all different.

Bricks

In the tranquil village of Waterfoot, Lancashire, lies the world's largest collection of bricks. Bricks of all shapes, sizes and uses are housed in two sheds and two garages owned by Henry Holt. Henry has been collecting bricks for over 21 years and his total on 22 January 1986 amounts to 3,454 different British bricks and 88 different foreign bricks. Henry's oldest and rarest brick is Roman and dates back to the year 12 BC.

Cacti

The world's largest privately-owned collection of cacti outside botanical gardens is owned by Charles Abbott of Exeter, Devon. On 19 February 1986, Charles's collection totalled 8,479. They are also the most pampered collection of cacti in the world! After a dormant winter in the greenhouse, Charles prepares his prize cacti for showing by taking them first for a Turkish bath, then down to his local hairdresser's for a shampoo and trim.

Chewing gum wrappers

The world's largest collection of chewing gum wrappers (nearly all the same!) is that owned by Mrs May Nuckley of St Leonards-on-Sea, West Sussex, with a total of 1,560 on 23 January 1987, amassed since May began chewing 'Freedent Gum' in November 1984.

Chimney pots

The world's largest collection of assorted chimney pots is one numbering 79, gathered by Geoff Weaver of Nercwys, Mold, Wales. Geoff is still building up a catalogue of his collection and would like to hear from other collectors worldwide.

China cats

For 13 years, mine hosts, Frank and Pansy, of the Coach and Horses Inn, Rillington, North Yorkshire, have been

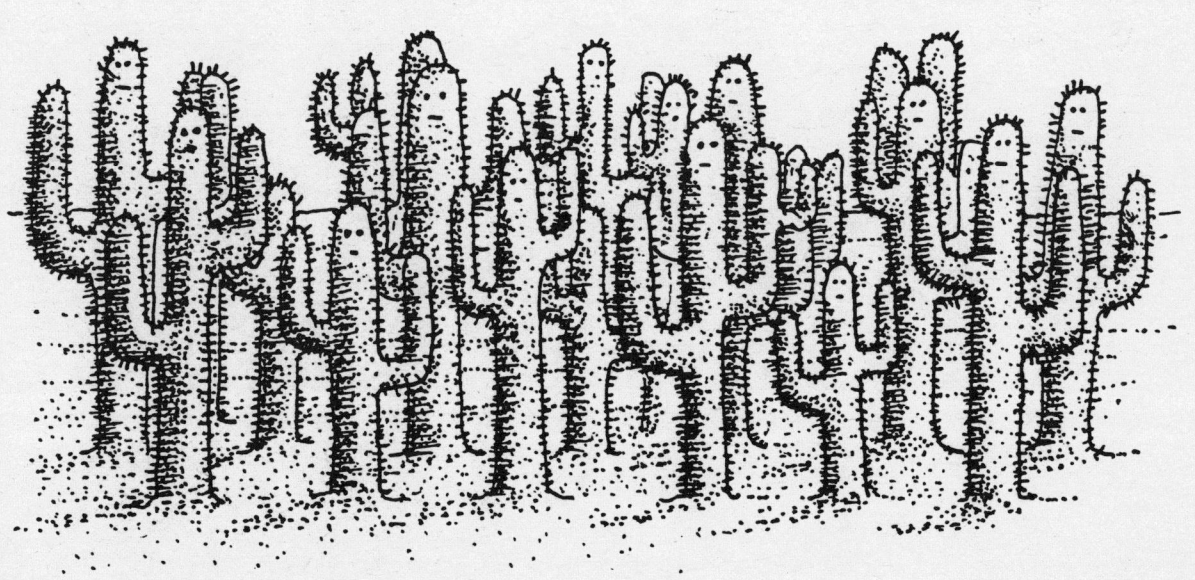

collecting china cats. Their collection can be seen in every room of the Inn and on 31 January 1986 totalled 743 cats, all different.

Cigar wrapper bands

Avid smoker Joseph Hruby of Lindhurst, Ohio, claims to have the world's largest collection of cigar bands, with a total of 175,500 up to 12 January 1987.

Comics

Do you remember those famous comics we all used to spend our pocket money on? *The Tiger*, *Jack and Jill*, *Eagle*, *Comic Cuts*. Dennis Gifford does. He's the proud owner of the world's largest collection of comics. Dennis, 59, of London, has been collecting comics from the age of 3. He now has over 15,498, all different; 96 are No 1 first editions.

Corkscrews

A recent claimant for the largest collection of corkscrews in the world is Richard Dennis of South Petherington, Somerset, with a total of 324, all different, as of 4 March 1987.

Dentures

The world's largest and tallest collection of broken dentures on permanent display is the two feet high mini-mountain owned by dentist Phil ('I hate VAT') Parsons of Hull, Humberside, with sets totalling over 100.

Dockland treasures

The largest privately-owned collection of dockland treasures is housed in the Hull barber shop of Mr Walter Oglesby.

With the decline in the general state of shipping and the associated docklands, Mr Oglesby began collecting his memorabilia only four years ago, yet it is now renowned throughout Europe for its quality and variety.

Of the 1,400 photographs, some dating back as far as 1880, most are of nostalgic value to his many visitors. Very shortly Walter might have to look for larger premises as the collection now comprises 38 different types of bag hook, 60 assorted hand hooks, and a vast array of blocks, spades, badges, books, official records, shovels, sieves, trolleys, satchels, tomahawks, ropeworkings and scoops.

In April 1987, Walter's collection proved invaluable to a local theatre company who required authentic relics of Hull dockers' implements for use in a semi-documentary play.

Erasers

A claim recently received from Sami Giles, 16 of Bayford, Somerset, details the fact that she has the world's largest collection of erasers, totalling 130, all different, on 12 April 1987.

GCEs

The greatest number of GCEs (General Certificate of Education) accumulated to date is 66, by Dr Francis L. Thomason of London. These are listed as 56 'O' (Ordinary) levels, 9 'A' (Advanced) levels and 1 'S' (Special) level. The greatest number of 'A' levels earned is 14 (from a total of 34 'O' levels, 14 'A' levels and 1 'S' level) by Albert F. Prime, whilst a detainee at HM Open Prison, Sudbury, between 1968 and 1982.

Key rings

The world's most avid copoclephologist is Mr Tracey White of Daytona, Whitington, Norfolk. His amazing collection of key rings totalled 3,108, all different, on 2 April 1987.

Knickers

Landlord of The Sperling Pound Gardens Pub, Norton, Stoke-on-Trent, Staffs, Mr Brian Prince is not claiming to have the world's largest collection of knickers, but he'd like to have! At 1 April 1987, Brian has accumulated only 36 pairs, mostly donated by his regulars, but if anybody wants to swell his collection, they'll be gratefully received.

Lego

The world's largest privately owned collection of Lego, 'just about one billion pieces', is housed in the London home of classical sculptor John Duffield. Among John's many spectacular creations have been a working cuckoo-clock, a 13 ft dinosaur that roars, and a life-size Arthur Scargill.

Marbles

Idris Jones of Swansea, West Glamorgan, is the new record holder for the world's largest collection of marbles. Although individual taws are obviously duplicated many times over, his collection totalled 5,618 on 29 January 1987.

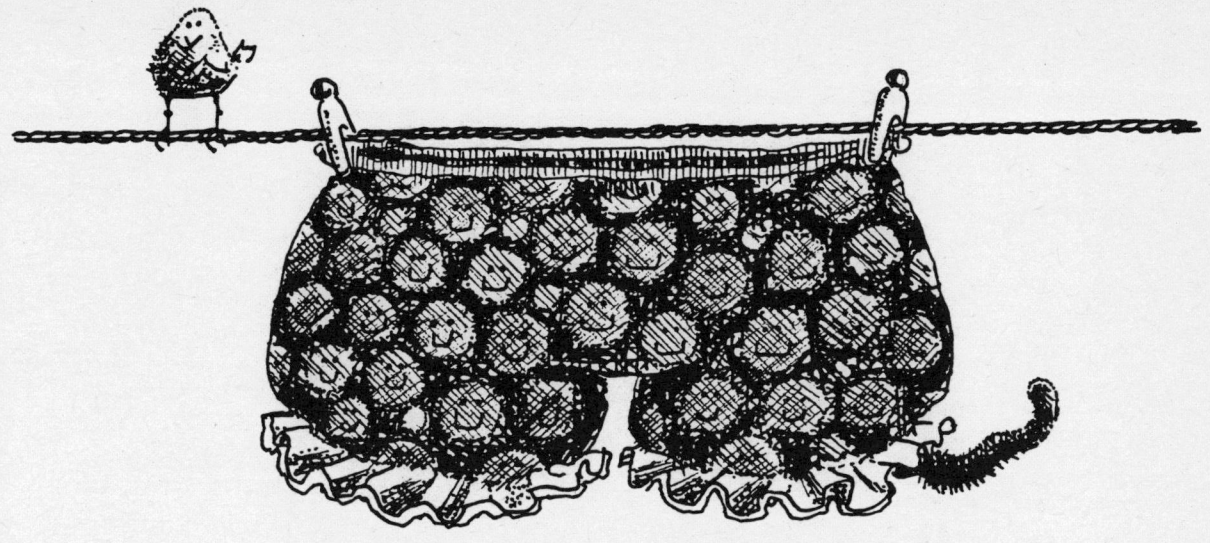

Miniature bottles

On 25 April 1986 it was reported that David Maund of Upham, Hampshire, had increased the size of his miniature bottle collection to 26,794, all different.

Model buses

Geoff and Linda Price and their family from Wednesbury, West Midlands, travel thousands of miles every year in search of new items to add to their collection of model buses and trams. Their collection is the largest one of its kind in the world and as of 1 February 1987 contained 3,011 different examples, valued at £55,000.

In October 1986, Geoff acquired his largest and most valuable model; a 10 ft Leyland Royal Tiger, built in 1951 and registered LUF 1. The working ⅓rd scale model seats six children and was discovered in a garage in Morecombe, Lancashire, where it had lain unused for 20 years.

Monopoly games

Monopoly fanatic Dr Peter Altman, 45, of Edgware, Middlesex, is nearing the end of his worldwide search which began 11 years ago from Platform Three of Fenchurch St Station. Peter is the proud owner of 33 sets of the property dealing board game Monopoly. The games have been collected from 29 different countries and are printed in 17 different languages. Peter lacks only one set in Hindi to complete the collection. Can anyone help?

Newspaper cuttings

As outlined in the introduction, I started on the road as a would-be writer by collecting snippets of information from radio, TV and newspapers. David Bowman of Pocklington, East Yorkshire, must now be well on the way to having enough information to write a library full of books. David has the world's largest collection of newspaper cuttings. On 1 January 1987 his files were crammed with 79,100 cuttings.

One-armed bandits

Humberside timber merchant John Gresham owns a one-armed bandit for every day of the year – 365 of them. The majority of them are kept at his home in North Dalton, but 115 are housed in a small display – 'Penny Arcadia' at Pocklington.

Packaging collection

The largest assortment of collected packaging is one hoarded over the past 23 years by Robert Opie, formerly of London, now residing near Bristol. Robert never throws anything away for fear that an important piece of history will be lost forever. At the age of 16, Robert was unwrapping a packet of his favourite sweets – 'Munchies' – when he realised that if he threw away the empty packet, he'd never see it again. From that moment's inspiration, Robert began to save everything. The collection of old tins, boxes, bottles, packets, etc, now totals more than 300,000 and includes some 5,800 yoghurt pots.

Pigs

The perfect porcinologist! That's probably the best description to apply to Mary Marsh of Edmonsham, Dorset. Mary has the world's largest collection of 'piggy-things'. On 2 February 1987 her collection totalled 507, including such items as piggy banks, jugs, toys, mugs, biscuit barrels, postcards and soap dishes.

Police equipment

The world's largest privately-owned collection of police equipment is housed in the home of ex-policeman Mervyn Mitton at Bournemouth, Dorset. This magnificent collection comprises over 2,000 different items including swords, uniforms, lamps, badges, helmets, handcuffs, leg irons, whistles, rule books and 410 finely decorated truncheons.

Racking taps

The recent welcome revival of traditional cask-conditioned ale has heralded an interest in the requisites associated with the old fashioned barrels. At the Shakespeare Inn, Hedon, Humberside, landlord Alexander ('Joan') Craig is claiming to have the world's largest collection of brass racking taps, which on 6 March 1986 totalled 36, all different.

Rolls-Royce

One of the most valuable collections of cars in the world was owned by Bhagwan Shree Rajneesh, head of the American based cult, 'The Orange People'.

The Bhagwan had a fervent passion for Rolls-Royce motor cars and had been presented with 82 of them – all 'Silver Spurs' – by his faithful followers before his deportation from the USA in 1985.

Rolls-Royce 'Silver Spurs' sell for about £91,000 each, making the total value of his collection around £7,462,000. Shortly after his

deportation the whole collection was sold to a millionaire car-dealer from Dallas, USA, for £3,500,000. Most of the vehicles had less than 500 miles on the clock.

Royal memorabilia

After watching the coronation of Queen Elizabeth II in 1953, Mrs Lesley Hirst of Lancaster started collecting Royal memorabilia. Since then she has expanded her collection to include 1,410 books, 487 pieces of chinaware, 4,917 postcards, 284 pitkins (small illustrated books), 60 commemorative tins and numerous assorted models, slides and commemorative magazines.

Shoes

The largest privately-owned collection of shoes in the world is in the possession of Mrs Lee Crome, aged 58, of Durham, North Carolina, USA. Lee has been collecting shoes since she was a 'young woman' and on 30 November 1985 had amassed a staggering 418 pairs.

Sugar bags

The world's largest collection of sugar bags belongs to Claire Henderson of the North Riding Hotel, Scarborough, North Yorkshire, with a total of 589, all different. Claire also collects sugar cube wrappers and has accumulated 193, all different.

Teddy Bears (infirm, elderly and unwanted)

Down and Out Teddies and Pandas have a haven and refuge at the home of sisters Barbara and Benita Brown of Malvern, Worcestershire. Among the 600 unwanted and dishevelled Teddies collected to date are Lady Elizabeth, who once belonged to the Queen Mother, and a ragged koala once owned by ex-Crossroads star, the late Noele Gordon.

Vacuum cleaners

The world's largest collection of manually operated vacuum cleaners, totalling 98, is owned by Swiss electronics engineer, Peter Frei, 35, of Duebendorf, Switzerland. Peter has only been collecting for four years and pays regular visits to England and the USA to add to his unique collection.

Chapter Three

GASTRONOMIC RECORDS

The most prolific of all record breakers is Peter Dowdeswell of Earls Barton, Northamptonshire. Peter's gastronomic achievements have brought him worldwide fame since he started his eating and drinking career back in 1974. Peter's money-raising sponsored events have earned over £80,000 for charity and his one-man shows are a true marvel to behold.

DRINKING

1 pint of beer in 0.45 seconds

1 pint of beer upside-down in 2.58 seconds

1 litre of beer in 1.30 seconds

1 litre of beer upside-down in 6.0 seconds

2 pints of beer in 2.30 seconds

2 pints of beer upside-down in 6.40 seconds

2½ pints 'yard of ale' in 5.0 seconds

3 pints of beer in 4.20 seconds

3 pints 'yard of ale' in 5.06 seconds

3½ pints 'yard of ale' in 5.44 seconds

4 pints of beer upside-down in 22.10 seconds

2 litres of beer in 6.0 seconds

2 litres of beer upside-down in 15.20 seconds

4 pints 'yard of ale' in 8.90 seconds

5 pints 'yard of ale' in 10.0 seconds

7½ pints 'yard of ale' in 14.0 seconds

One gallon of beer upside-down in 8 min 35 sec

Twelve pints of beer whilst Big Ben was striking twelve o'clock (Big Ben had just struck 8 when Peter finished)

1 pint of champagne upside-down in 3.30 seconds

3½ pints 'yard of champagne' in 14.20 seconds

2 pints of milk in 3.20 seconds

34 pints of beer in 1 hour

90 pints of beer in 3 hours

EATING

Cheese: 1 lb of Cheddar in 1 min 13 sec

Doughnuts: 45 two-hole in 17 min 32 sec

Eels: 1 lb of elvers in 13.7 seconds

Eggs, hard boiled: 14 in 41.57 seconds

Eggs, raw: 13 from a glass in 1.4 seconds

Eggs, soft boiled: 38 in 1 min 15 sec

Fish & Chips: 4 lb fish plus 4 lb chips in 5 min 42 sec

Gherkins: 1 lb in 27.20 seconds

Grapes: 3 lb in 31.10 seconds

Haggis: 1 lb 10 oz in 49.05 seconds

Hamburgers: 21, each 3½ oz, including buns, in 9 min 42 sec

Ice Cream (partly thawed): 12 lb in 45.5 seconds

Jam Sandwiches: 40, each 6 in × 3¾ in × 1½ in, in 17 min 53 sec

Jelly: 20 fluid oz in solid form with a dessert spoon in 8.25 seconds

Mashed Potatoes: 3 lb in 1 min 22 sec

Meat Pies: 22, each 5½ oz, in 18 mins 13.3 sec

Pancakes: 62, each six inches in diameter, buttered and with syrup in 6 min 58 sec

Pizza: 3 lb in 2 minutes exactly

Porridge: 6 lb in 2 min 34 sec

Prunes: 144 in 34 seconds

Ravioli: 5 lb in 5 min 34 sec

Sausages: 96, each 1 oz, in 4 min 29 sec

Scrambled Eggs: 30 in 45.0 seconds

Shrimps: 3 lb in 3 min 10 sec

Spaghetti: 100 yds in 12.02 seconds

Spaghetti Bolognese: 1 lb, including sauce, in 32.0 seconds

Strawberries: 2 lb in 12.95 seconds
and 2 lb 8 oz in 27.19 seconds
Sushi (raw fish & rice): 1 lb 8 oz in 1
min 13 sec

When Peter retires (if ever he does) the Dowdeswell name should still be perpetuated as his son, Tony, and his son-in-law, Shaun Barry, are also champion guzzlers and their feats are recorded elsewhere in this chapter.

Peter Dowdeswell is not the only world champion eater and drinker featured in this chapter; hosts of other gastronomes are claiming their rightful recognition.

Baby's bottle of beer

The landlord of Ye Old White Harte pub in Hull, Humberside, is a real sucker. Derrick Sykes holds the world record for the shortest time taken to drink half a pint of ale from a baby's bottle. On 19 April 1985, Derrick was timed at 3 min 38.62 sec.

Baked beans

Toilet attendant Kerry White holds the world record for the greatest number of baked beans consumed in 24 hours, with a total of 12,547. The beans were eaten individually with a cocktail stick and the record was created at Weymouth, Dorset, on 20 August 1984.

On 4 April 1984, Karen Stevenson of Wallasey, Merseyside, ate 2,780 cold baked beans individually with a cocktail stick in 30 minutes.

'Barnsley Chops'

Four 'Barnsley Chops', eight Yorkshire puddings, eight roast potatoes and trimmings (total 8½ lbs) were eaten in 40 minutes by Alan Newbold at the Queen's Hotel, Barnsley, Yorkshire, on 4 April 1981.

Barrel of beer

The shortest recorded time in which a 9 gallon barrel of ale has been consumed is 2 hr 14 min 56.96 sec by a team of six: Derrick Sykes (14), Alan Benstead (13), Chris Bentley (12), Innis Belcher (11), Bill Simmons (11), Dave Watson (11) at Ye Olde White Harte, Hull, Humberside, on 27 May 1986. The figures in brackets represent the number of pints consumed – not their ages!

Beer – female records

The following records for consumption of beer by a woman are held by Mrs Connie Dowdeswell of Earls Barton, Northants:

1 pint of beer in 2.10 seconds
1 pint of beer upside-down in 5.20
seconds

At The Catholic Club, Hoyland, Barnsley, Yorkshire, on 18 April 1986, Samantha Micklethwaite drank a pint of beer through a 4 mm straw in 42.63 seconds.

Beer through a straw

This category now relates to four different sized straws being used in pubs and clubs.

3 mm diameter: 25.07 seconds by Patrick Tyler at the Ponsmere Hotel, Perranporth, Cornwall, on 14 July 1983.

4 mm diameter: 24.03 seconds by Tony Wildsmith at the Catholic Club, Hoyland, Yorkshire, on 18 April 1986.

6 mm diameter: 11.60 seconds by Peter Dowdeswell at the Boat Inn, Earls Barton, Northants on 14 March 1985.

8 mm diameter: 9.63 seconds by Keith Medforth at the Four in Hand, Hull, Humberside on 21 February 1987.

Beer with a teaspoon

On 26 November 1985, Derrick Sykes drank a pint of beer with a teaspoon in 1 min 45.62 sec on BBC Television's 'Breakfast Time', Chief scrutineer was presenter Frank Bough, who tried to claim a reward of one of Derrick's front teeth, which was knocked out during the record breaking attempt.

Black pudding

On 17 January 1986, Arthur Wilson, 28, of Macclesfield, Cheshire, set a new world record for eating boiled black pudding by scoffing 3 lb 4 oz in 8 min 56.8 sec.

The largest black pudding ever made was 1,600 metres long, weighing 2,000 kilograms. It was eaten by 18,000 people at a festival in Barcelona, Spain, on 15 September 1986.

Cabbage

When ex-greengrocer Alf Minter decided to emigrate to Canada in April 1980, he was presented with a farewell present by some of his London colleagues: a 3 lb cabbage and a packet of seeds to plant in his new homestead. Unfortunately, export regulations forbade the carrying of either of the gifts without prior permission from the Ministry of Agriculture, Fisheries and Food. Determined to take his mementoes with him, Alf seated himself in the Lounge Bar at Heathrow Airport and ate the lot. The seeds were swallowed first, followed by the cabbage which took just under 30 minutes to devour.

Cannibals (British)

During the fifteenth century the cannibalistic, cave-dwelling Beane Family from Galloway, Scotland, are reported to have murdered and eaten more than 1,000 victims over a 20-year period. Their numbers were ever on the increase as Chief Clansman, Sawney Beane, his wife, 14 children, 18 grandchildren and 14 great-

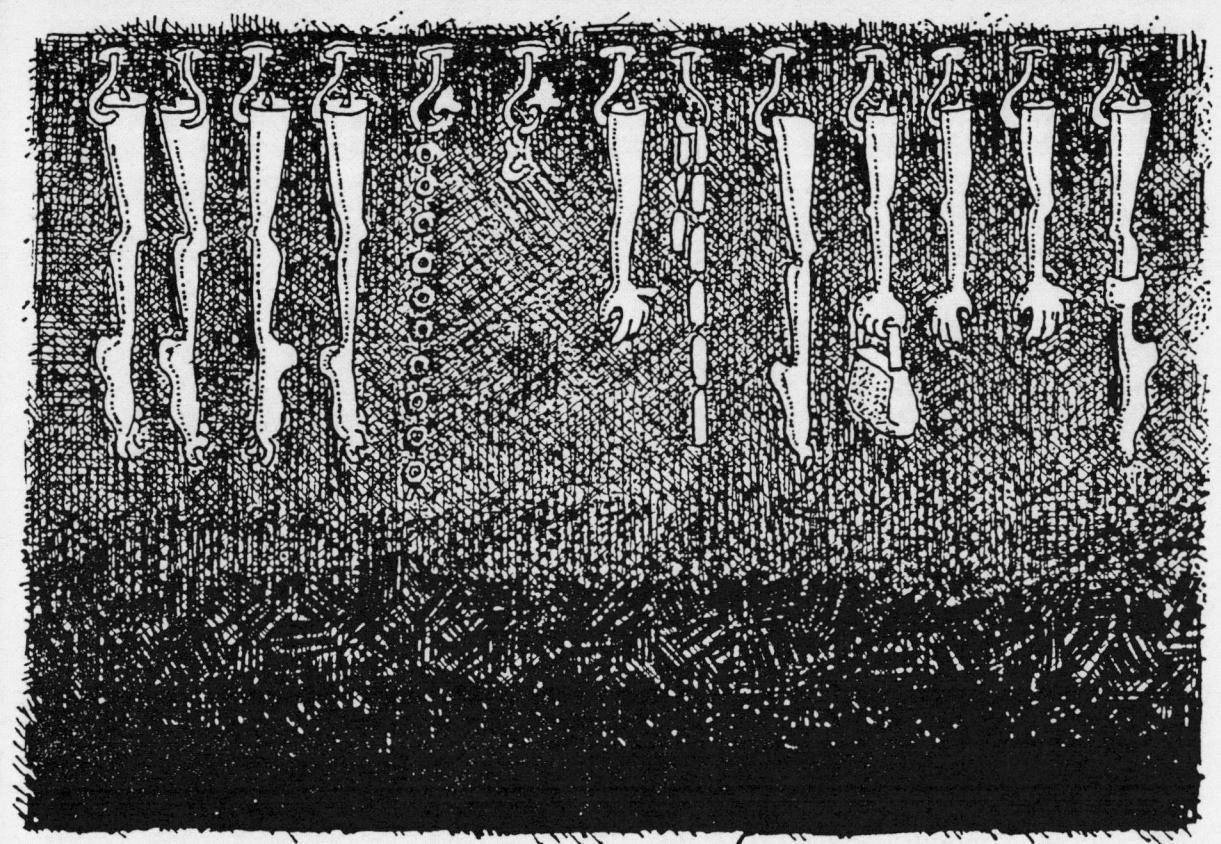

grandchildren thrived and prospered on the loot and flesh of unfortunate travellers.

In 1435 one of their intended victims escaped from their camp and was able to bring an army of 400 troops, led by King James I himself, back to their hide-out. There the King found scores of victims pickled and festooning the walls like a butcher's shop. The whole family were rounded up and taken to Edinburgh and slowly and painfully tortured and *executed en masse* without trial.

Capsicum (Red Peppers)

John 'Hot Lips' Hancock, 28, guzzled his way through three pounds of raw capsicums at Macon County Fair, Georgia, USA, on 1 August 1982. No time was recorded.

Carrots

The fastest time ever recorded to munch through one kilogram of raw carrots is 11 min 14 sec by Geoff Porter of Shaftesbury, Dorset, on 17 April 1986.

The longest and heaviest carrot ever

grown was by Ken Ayliffe at Bronllys, Mid Wales, measuring 9 ft 10 in and weighing 10 lb 7 oz on 28 September 1986.

Champagne

Mine host at the Black Raven Inn, London, Bobby Acland, claims to drink an average of 3 bottles of champagne every day – 1,095 per annum. At an average of £6 per bottle (wholesale) it makes Bobby the world's biggest annual spender on alcohol.

Chicken

The fastest recorded time taken to eat 3 lb 12 oz of boneless chicken meat is 8 min 5 sec by Shaun Barry, 25, at the Royal Oak, Bishops Cleeve, Cheltenham, Gloucestershire, on 5 July 1986.

Chow (dog)

At the Happy Valley Football Stadium, Hong Kong, on 19 September 1980, Lim Ho Wong consumed 3½ lb of cooked dog meat in 18 min 10 sec.

Cider through a straw

The fastest recorded time that a pint of cider has been drunk through a straw (no more than 6 mm in diameter) is 19.05 seconds by Derrick Sykes at Ye Olde White Harte, Hull, Humberside, on 8 September 1985.

Cockles

Tony Dowdeswell, 19, downed two pints of cockles in 1 min 0.08 sec at the Corby Stardust Bingo Hall, on 14 February 1985.

Cockroaches

At the 'Alternative Olympics', Hull, on 31 August 1986, Ken Edwards set a new world record by eating 28 cockroaches in four minutes.

Cottage cheese

Dr Peter Altman of Edgware, Middlesex, holds the world record for eating cottage cheese with a tablespoon. He gobbled down exactly 3 lb in 4 minutes on 4 March 1984.

Cream crackers

The fastest recorded time that 20 dry 'Jacob's' cream crackers have been eaten is 10 min 42.8 sec by Terry Smith at the Tower Nightclub, Hull, Humberside, on 9 November 1986.

The speed record for devouring three dry 'Jacob's' cream crackers is 32.28 seconds by Shirley ('Bubbles') Allerston at M. F. Snooker Centre, Hull on 31 October 1986.

Crisps

It has been reliably reported that Paul Tully of Brisbane University gobbled down 30 two ounce bags of crisps, without a drink, in 24 min 33.6 sec on 6 May 1969.

The largest bag of crisps ever made was to celebrate the wedding of HRH Prince Charles to Lady Diana Spencer in 1981, by the Scunthorpe firm, Sooner Foods. No weight was ever recorded but the bag measured 119 ft 4½ inches in length.

Cucumber

On 11 December 1983, Ernst Muller, 26, of Hamburg, West Germany, consumed one kilogram of raw, unsliced cucumber in 4 min 14.60 sec.

Custard

At the Catholic Club, Hoyland, Yorkshire, Alan Newbold drank four one-pint mugs of cold custard in the record time of 1 min 36.05 sec on 18 April 1986.

Daffodils

At the Queen's Head, Burley in Wharfedale, on 31 March 1972, Pauline Lambert, 30, devoured 60 fresh daffodil heads in 14 min 28.5 sec.

Dogs' dinner

On 8 September 1985, 506 dogs wolfed down 200 lb of meat and 100 lb of biscuits in exactly ten minutes at Ragley Hall, Alcester, Warwickshire.

Earthworms

The record consumption of cooked worms (killed by chloroform and boiled for five minutes), each averaging 7 in long and ¼ in thick, is 53, in 3 min 40 sec by Alan Newbold of Barnsley, on 4 February 1985.

Eels

The fastest recorded time that 1,000 elvers have been eaten (approximate weight 2 lb) is 21.2 seconds by Mark Ryder, 24, at the annual world championships at Gloucester, on 8 April 1985.

Eggs

The following egg records are all held by Alan Newbold of Barnsley, Yorkshire:

RAW
36 raw eggs from a 'yard of ale' glass in 17.0 seconds.
50 raw eggs from four one-pint mugs in 28.20 seconds.
30 raw eggs from two one-pint mugs in 10.30 seconds.

HARD BOILED
54 in 15 minutes exactly (without a drink).

Fondue

On 15 August 1984, 15 chefs made the biggest cheese fondue in the world, using 413.6 lb of cheese, 154 bottles of white wine, two bottles of Kirsch liqueur,

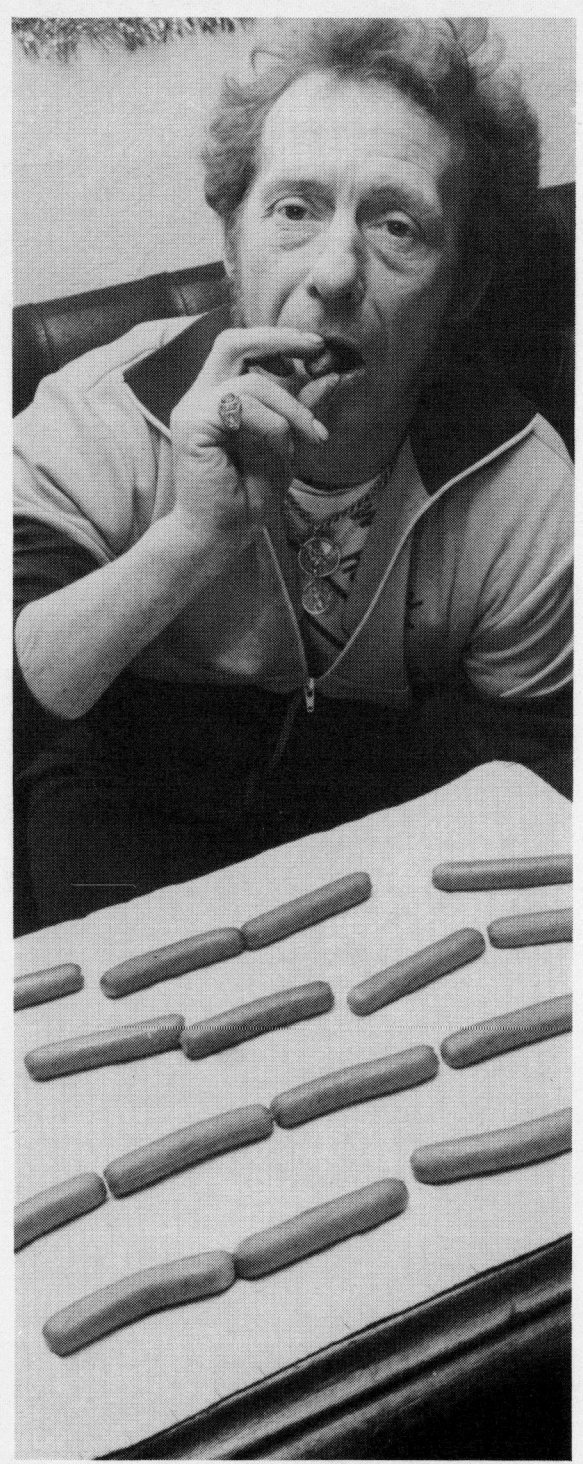

9 lb of garlic and 1 lb of mushrooms. Over 1,500 guests sat down in St Gervais, France, to dunk 32,000 pieces of bread into the gigantic dish of melted cheese which had been cooked in a 1,500 litre cauldron over a wood fire.

Foxy boozer

A young fox cub kept by Ralph Barnett of Little Downham, Cambridgeshire, holds the foxy boozer record for drinking half a pint of beer from a bowl in 43 seconds.

Frankfurters

At the Pear Tree Inn, Brownhills, West Midlands, on 9 December 1985, Reg Morris set a new frankfurter eating record by devouring 24.2 ounces of frankfurters in 1 min 15.5 sec.

Grass

After losing a bet to a fellow young farmer, Paul Shaw of Swindon, Wiltshire, was forced to pay the penalty. He ate 16 ounces of fresh grass mowings, using only a knife and fork, in 15 min 0.05 sec on 22 May 1968.

Hot cross buns

On 9 April 1971, during the interlude at a pop concert in Cathedral Square, Peterborough, Walter Cornelius ate ten 10 oz hot cross buns in 5 min 10 sec.

Ice cream

The shortest time taken to eat 3 lb 6 oz of unmelted ice cream with a spoon is 31.67 seconds by Tony Dowdeswell, 21, in New York, USA, on 16 July 1986.

Kippers

Reg Morris of Brownhills, West Midlands, shattered the world kipper eating record on 1 November 1985 by scoffing 27 (self-filleted) kippers. He devoured a total weight of 16 lb 15 oz in 35 min 24 sec at the Woolpack, Short Heath, West Midlands.

Lager through a straw

This category now relates to four different sized straws being used in pubs and clubs.

3 mm diameter: 32.39 seconds by Derrick Sykes at BBC TV's Pebble Mill Studio, Birmingham, on 19 November 1985.

4 mm diameter: 28.62 seconds by Alec Liddle at Patrington Haven, Humberside, on 9 July 1986.

6 mm diameter: 11.50 seconds by Peter Hanson at Birmingham Students' Carnival, Birmingham, on 16 November 1985.

8 mm diameter: 11.02 seconds by Horrace Forge at The Red Lion, Norwich, on 17 April 1986.

Lager with a teaspoon

At Birmingham Students' Carnival Rag on 16 November 1985, Steve Stringer set a new lager drinking record by slurping down a pint with a teaspoon in 3 min 36 sec.

Lamb roll

The longest lamb roll in the world measuring 32 ft 10 in was stuffed by David Jenkins of Scunthorpe on 6 August 1972 with 28 pounds of seasoning in 4½ hours.

Maggots

The fastest recorded time taken to eat 100 live maggots individually without a drink (or being sick) is 5 min 32 sec by Reg Morris of Brownhills, West Midlands, on 29 January 1986.

Monsieur Mangetout

Frenchman Michel Lotito uses the name 'Monsieur Mangetout' (Mr Eatall) to describe quite aptly his feats of gastronomic omnivorousness. Since the age of 16, Michel has astounded friends and his doctors by eating:

Eight bicycles, one of them in the record time of 10 days.
Seven TV sets.
80 ft of steel chain.
One supermarket trolley in the record time of 4½ days.

One full Cessna light aircraft whilst working in Caracas, Venezuela.
One 6 ft 6 in × 3 ft coffin.
One 'Black Beret' milk shake in 2½ mins.

The metal was all ground and cut into filings and the rubber, plastic and fabric chopped up and boiled before being swallowed. Unless you've got a lead-lined stomach and the constitution of a Sherman tank, don't attempt to beat these records!

Olives

Constantine Hadgipatterus of Yannina, Greece, is the world champion olive eater with a tally of 150 (stoned and stuffed) in 16 min 02.2 sec achieved on 17 February 1986.

Onions

On 18 December 1979, Walter Cornelius of Peterborough, Cambridgeshire, shattered the world record for eating raw onions by downing 3 lb 8 oz in 2 min 2 sec.

Oysters

The most prodigious feat of consuming shelled oysters was achieved by American Tommy Greene on 6 July 1985. In Annapolis, Maryland, USA, he slurped 288 of them weighing a total of six pounds in 1 min 33.5 sec.

Peas

Intrepid pea-eater Simon Escreet set a new world record on 2 February 1985 at Ye Olde White Harte, Hull, Humberside, by devouring 500 tinned peas, singly, with a cocktail stick, in 19 min 2.56 sec.

The fastest recorded time for devouring 100 peas in a similar fashion is 1 min 56.3 sec by Criss Drysdale of Alsger, Staffordshire, at Birmingham University Carnival on 16 November 1985.

Pie – largest

Put all the gargantuan, gastronomic trenchermen and women together, give them a week to complete the task, then ask them to eat the biggest pie ever made. It's a 10 to 1 chance that they won't get remotely close.

The largest pie ever made was produced in 1964 in the Yorkshire village of Denby Dale, to celebrate four royal births.

The ingredients consisted of:

3 tons of prime English beef
1½ tons of potatoes
½ ton of gravy and seasoning
½ ton of flour
¼ ton of lard.

Pineapple

The fastest recorded time for eating a 2 lb pineapple, skin and all (but not the green top), is 3 min 33.4 sec by Dave Walton of Newcastle, Tyne & Wear, on 17 December 1974.

Pizza

World champion pizza eater and record holder is Michael Peacock of Peterborough, who munched his way through a 12 inch diameter pizza weighing 2 lb in the time of 2 min 54.82 sec on 28 April 1986.

Port

Reports from various sources claim that at a charity banquet in London, Dr Samuel Johnson (1709–84) drank 36 glasses of port in three hours, without leaving the table once.

Porter

Walter Cornelius drank three consecutive three-pint 'yards' of porter in 39.9 seconds at the Dolphin, Peterborough, on 20 September 1971.

Prunes

The most prodigious feat of prune eating was performed by Alan Newbold of Barnsley, who demolished 150 with a tablespoon in exactly 31 seconds at 'Bassetts', Sheffield, Yorkshire, on 4 February 1984.

'Hungry' Reg Morris ate 144 prunes using his fingers in 33.44 seconds at the

Saddler Centre, Walsall, West Midlands, on 1 March 1986.

Punch

On 25 October 1694 in Alicante, Spain, six thousand officers and men of the Royal Navy got pie-eyed when Admiral Sir Edward Russell ordered the largest punch ever made to be brewed in a gigantic marble bowl. Four hogsheads of brandy (80 casks), one pipe (105 gallons) of Malaga wine, 20 gallons of lime juice, 1,300 lb of fine white sugar, 5 lb of grated nutmeg and 9 casks of water were stirred together. A canopy was placed over the massive bowl to prevent the punch from evaporating and a cabin boy rowed around on a small raft on top of the brew serving the increasingly merry sailors. The cabin boys had to be replaced every 15 minutes when the fumes went to their heads.

Rice

Goanese merchant seaman Parbatinath Basu is the world champion boiled rice eater. At Visakapatnam, India, on 24 December 1970, he downed 2 lb 8 oz in 17 min 11 sec using only his fingers – and left not one solitary grain.

Richard Fuller

Nobody is claiming a record for eating Richard Fuller; I just thought I'd give him a mention.

Richard Fuller of Witham, Essex, is the world's foremost authority on Alternative Appetite Control and is head of Crackpot College. Since 1974, Richard has extolled the virtues of his favourite slimming aid – cardboard. 'Each mouthful should be chewed just 60 times,' he says, 'but don't swallow it . . . just use it as a food substitute and those pounds of unwanted fat will quickly fall away.'

Round of drinks

The biggest round of drinks ever paid for was one costing $1,500 for 1,501 people (a dollar a head and his own drink was free) by Paul Deer at U-Zoo and Co, Atlanta, Georgia, USA, on 14 July 1982.

Sandwich

The largest sandwich ever made (beef, cheese and salad) was by Sutton's Bakery, Coventry, West Midlands, on 6 April 1986. It was 600 feet in length and weighed 565 lb.

Sausages

The greatest number of cooked one ounce sausages consumed in one hour is 122½ by Joe Blackie of Edinburgh at his local pub, The Norhet, on 14 January 1983.

The following sausage eating records are all held by the late Walter Cornelius of Peterborough, Cambridgeshire.

47 two ounce (raw) in 8 min 30 sec at Cathedral Square, Peterborough, on 11 April 1972.

30 two ounce (hot) in 10 min 11.8 sec at Peterborough Motor Show Rooms on 8 May 1969.

60 two ounce (cold) in 8 min 58.8 sec at Peterborough Motor Show Rooms on 26 July 1969.

17 ft 6 in chain of raw, two ounce sausages (total weight 5 lb) in 5 min 34 sec at Peterborough Municipal Swimming Baths on 22 June 1979.

Shredded Wheat (in a wheelbarrow)

A team of six (three sitting and eating and three pushing) from the MENCAP association have succeeded where the famous have failed. Whilst being pushed around a course measuring one mile at Gravesend, Kent, on 9 September 1984, the team consumed a total of 43 shredded wheat in a time of 15 minutes exactly.

Slugs

Only one man would have the nerve, tenacity and stomach to set a world record for eating live slugs – 'Ratman' Ken Edwards of Hyde, Cheshire. Ken set his record at a local carnival in 1982 by eating 12 slugs in two minutes. As a dessert he ate two brillo pads.

Smorgasbord

Smorgasbord is a Scandinavian open sandwich. The largest smorgasbord ever made was 400 yards long with fillings of reindeer, salmon and herrings, on a specially constructed table in the suburbs of Stockholm, Sweden.

On 31 May 1984, 30,000 record breaking revellers each tucked into a piece.

Snails

On 14 August 1985, American Tommy Greene ate one kilogram (2.2 lb) of snails in 2 min 43.2 sec at Hamilton's Brasserie, London.

Spaghetti

The fastest recorded time for consuming 125 yards of spaghetti plus sauce from a four pint container is 8.61 seconds by Alan Newbold of Barnsley at Ye Olde White Harte, Hull, Humberside on 2 April 1986.

At an 'eatathon' staged at the Brumby Hotel, Scunthorpe, Humberside, on 22 June 1978, a team of 20 from Scunthorpe Rugby Club ate 42 lb of spaghetti with chopsticks in 20 minutes.

Sprouts

On 26 October 1981, Fred Kay, 28, from Trowbridge, Wiltshire, consumed three pounds of cooked brussels sprouts individually, using only a knitting needle, in 19 min 6 sec.

Suet pudding

4½ lb of suet pudding topped with a ½ gallon of custard was the dessert served up to Alan Newbold of Barnsley, Yorkshire, at the Drop, Addiston. Alan gobbled up the lot in 18 minutes exactly on 17 July 1983.

Sultanas

The fastest recorded time in which 100 sultanas have been devoured, singly, using only a cocktail stick is 1 min 44.65 sec by Mark Say of Selly Oak, Birmingham, on 16 November 1985.

Tea drinking

Newly acclaimed world champion tea drinker is Mrs Pat Crowther of Sheffield, Yorkshire. Pat's daily intake is a confirmed 70 cups of tea (2½ gallons), each laced with between three and five spoonfuls of sugar.

Tripe and onions

At the 1952 trades fair at Banbury, Oxfordshire, on 17 April, before a crowd of 2,000 people, Tommy McCourt, 26, gobbled down two pounds of tripe together with half a pound of onions in 12 minutes exactly.

Water melons

The fastest recorded time for eating five water melons (total weight seven pounds) is 8 min 30 sec by Reg Morris at The Woolpack, Short Heath, West Midlands, on 4 September 1985.

Wurzel

Eric McKenzie must be a scarecrow hater, for on 22 September 1980 he ate a 2 lb 6 oz raw wurzel in 22 min 14 sec at The White Horse Inn, Cheltenham, Gloucester.

Yorkshire pudding

John Davidson, 29, of Gainsborough, Lincolnshire, recently laid claim to a new world record for eating Yorkshire pudding, by wolfing three pounds plus half a pint of onion gravy in 7 min 22 sec on 18 March 1986.

Would you believe, the largest Yorkshire pudding ever made was in York! Yes, strangely enough, on 1 August 1985, on the Knavesmire, a pudding measuring 25 ft 3 in x 4 ft was baked using 44 dozen eggs, 87 lb flour and 29 gallons of milk.

Chapter Four

THE AMAZING WILF LUNN

Wilfred Makepeace Lunn was born at a very young age in Brighouse, West Yorkshire, on 20 March 1942. As far back as he can remember, Wilf was always active in the role of an inventor, but in his early years as a pupil at Hipperholme Grammar School he was a boy to beware.

Wilf's favourite pastime was setting booby traps for his friends and fellow pupils. He'd think nothing of connecting a trip wire to anything that would pop up and frighten the unsuspecting victims: buckets of whitewash, a decapitated chicken and even the odd homemade 'bomb'. (Potentially dangerous but never harmful!) Indeed Wilf's first real invention was a flour-bomb box. The box containing rods, levers, springs and of course a liberal amount of flour was left in conspicuous places sporting the label 'Do not open'. Now, surprisingly enough, very few people disobeyed these instructions, but those curious few who did were plastered with flour from head to toe.

Wilf left Hipperholme Grammar School in 1958 and for four years studied textile design at the Huddersfield School of Art, where he learned a great deal about the sophistication of design and adaptation to finished article. This grounding has since helped in the sometimes complex presentation of Wilf's mobile inventions.

In 1962, Wilfred Makepeace Lunn (as he then preferred to be known) embarked upon a career totally divorced from the profession for which he had been trained. He began teaching lip-reading to deaf children in the schools surrounding the town of Huddersfield. As a second vocation he also taught Religious Instruction. The aforementioned two skills finally gave way to his more creative vein and Wilf was pleased to impart his knowledge of art and pottery to similarly aged audiences.

In those heady days in the early and mid-sixties there was a general movement (some say sparked off by the Beatles and the Maharishi Mahesh Yogi) towards self-realisation and self-expression. In his own way Wilf had developed a unique skill of making miniature bikes. In fact he claims the

world record for being the first person to put a 'bike in a bottle'.

It was this particular skill which first brought his talents into public view by way of mass media coverage with an exhibition of his art-forms at Ansells Gallery in London. There followed features on radio and television and a resident guest spot on Independent Television's 'Magpie' as a 'Smoothing Iron and Pop Bottle Expert'. Another noteworthy accolade was as resident inventor on Tony Hart's 'Vision-on' – a programme of general interest which devoted special attention to the deaf.

A couple of years ago Wilf decided it was time that the Americans had a taste of his own brand of inventive art. He packed his bags and went to Boston, Massachusetts. In Wilf's own words, 'I went to America, but when I got there it was shut!' The main reason for this was that he had picked the unfortunate fortnight when hurricane Gloria was ravaging the eastern seaboard causing panic and destruction on a wholesale basis. 'Ever tried boiling water on a bar-b-que?' Wilf went on. 'Bloody impossible, but that's all we had; there was no electricity, no gas, no nothing. I didn't stay long.'

Now firmly ensconced back in dear old Blighty, Wilf Lunn lives in a semi-rural part of Huddersfield overlooking an expanse of natural parkland. His studio-house is bedecked with a hoard of unusual antiques which would defy classification by all but the best experts. But all would-be prowlers heed my words! There are all manner of booby

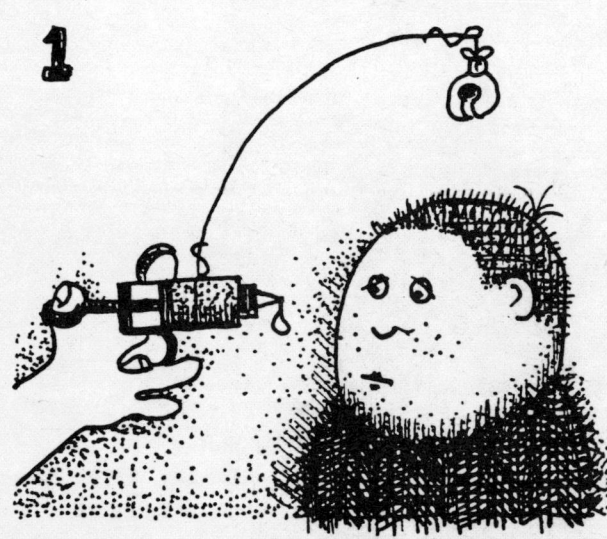

SHAKE BELL OVER HEAD

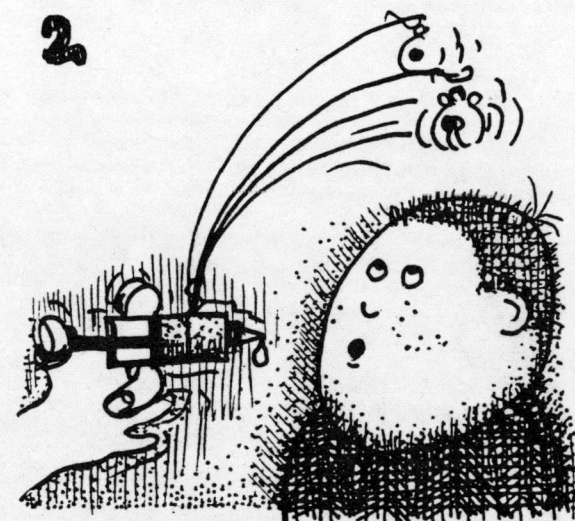

BABY LOOKS UP

traps and explosive devices littered throughout the grounds and in the house itself. Access to the Lunn residence is by invitation only. Anyone who doesn't heed this warning had better be well insured!

Wilf's one time hobby has now turned into a full time profession. In his own words, 'Life is now one long hobby.' He classes himself as a 'Biz-artist' and claims to have developed a new school of art – 'The Expensivist'.

To illustrate the latter he will, if required, make you a bike in a bottle for £60. For £120 he'll make you a bike in a bottle but remove it for you before you get it. Being a man of compromise he'll go one step further and make you a bike half-way into a bottle for £90.

Wilf Lunn's art-form inventions are now in constant demand by architects, companies and private individuals alike and a list of the famous and titled people on his customer list would more than fill this page. His most recent and longest commission is now housed in a pub in Newcastle-upon-Tyne. Appropriately named 'Inventions', the pub sports a working art-form entitled 'The Water Pond Heron Scarer and Lark Lure'.

The spacious workshop beneath Wilf's studio-house has spawned hundreds of bizarre and some might think eccentric inventions, but Wilf's favourite is extremely simple and guaranteed (nearly always) to work. This favourite invention is entitled 'The Sneaky Baby Feeder'. (See illustration.) Sneaky? Maybe! Ingenious? Definitely.

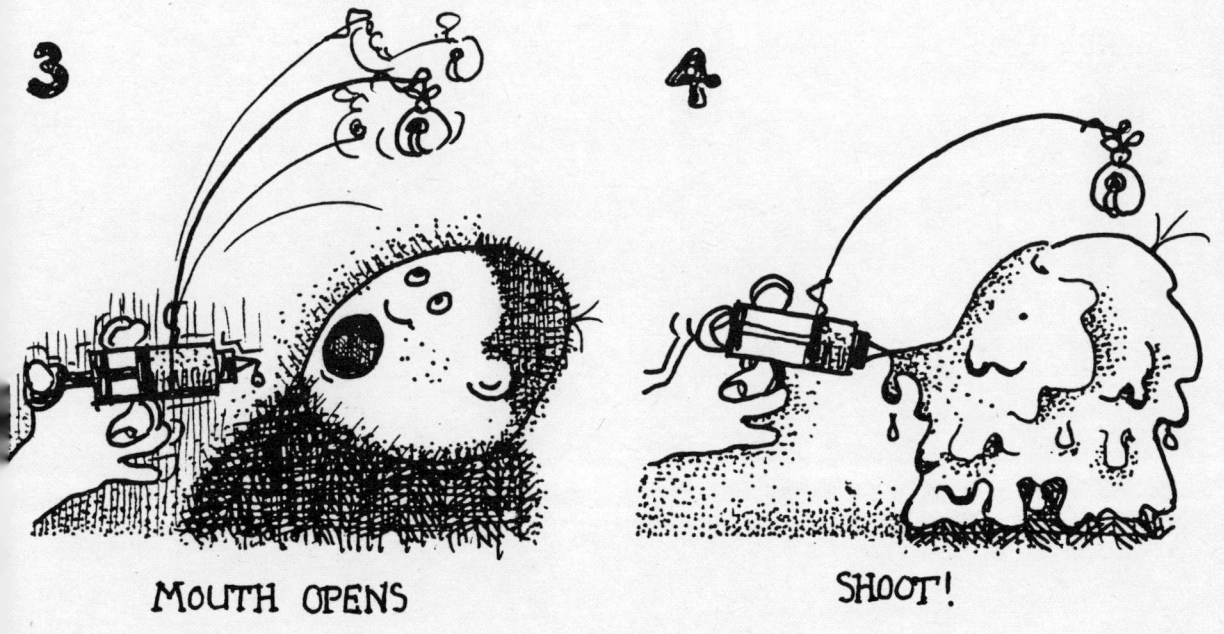

3 MOUTH OPENS

4 SHOOT!

Wilf Lunn appears to have complete contentment in his life, yet he still has his sights set on further achievement. His next project is to be the making of a series of short, silent movies featuring a wide selection of his mobile inventions. I for one can't wait for that project to be realised.

Chapter Five

SPORTING RECORDS

Abseiling

The longest abseil descent down the side of a man-made structure is one of 484 ft by Police Constable Gil Boyd of the Cambridgeshire Constabulary. As a tribute to his late partner Bob Reynolds, and as a fund raising stunt for the Hospital for Sick Children, Great Ormond Street, London, Gil abseiled down the side of the Post Office Tower, London, on 3 June 1985.

Aerobatics

On 23 August 1980, circling Houston International Raceways, Texas, USA, John McClain flew in an upside-down position for a total of 4 hr 9 min 5 sec in his Swick Taylorcraft.

Thirty-five-year-old pilot Ken Ballinger of Painswick, Gloucester, claimed the world record for looping the loop on 6 September 1983. He performed 155 loops in one hour over Staverton Airport, Cheltenham, Gloucester.

Aeroplane landing

The only known exponent of the art of landing an aeroplane atop a moving lorry is American stunt man Art Shorn of California, USA. Guided by a fellow stunt man, Larry Hall, Art landed his Piper J3 Club aircraft on the top of the lorry's 40 ft container unit travelling at a speed of 55 mph.

Alternative circuit training

Most sporting and health clubs have set standards of circuit training (performing several disciplines in a set time). The alternative circuit training disciplines are:

1. Breaking in half a six inch nail.
2. Tearing in half a telephone directory.
3. Performing 60 dips on the parallel bars with two seven pound weights tied to the legs.

The current record holder is Fred Burton, who completed all the disciplines in 1 min 41.5 sec at the Cheadle Activities Club, Cheadle, Staffs, on 12 May 1985.

American football

The greatest number of points scored by a professional 'grid-iron' player is 2,002 in a career spanning 26 years (1949–75) by George Blanda, whose four clubs were Chicago Bears, Baltimore, Houston and Oakland.

Recent tests on the Dallas Cowboy's running back, Herschel Walker, have confirmed that he holds the world record for having the lowest percentage body fat of any athlete. His 220 lb body has only an astonishing 1.42 per cent fat, whereas the average for league players is 11 per cent.

Atlantic crossing

Built by Brooke Yachts Ltd of Lowestoft, Suffolk, in only 21 weeks, The Virgin Atlantic Challenger II, skippered by Richard Branson, made the fastest ever crossing of the Atlantic Ocean by a mono-hulled vessel in the record time of 80 hr 31 min.

Virgin Atlantic Challenger II left the Ambrose Light Tower off the coast of New York State, USA, at 10.03 Greenwich Mean Time on 26 June 1985. The vessel, intact with a crew of six (Richard Branson, Chay Blyth, Dag Pike, Steve Ridgway, Peter Macann, Eckhard Rastig), crossed the finishing line – Bishop's Rock Lighthouse, Isles of Scilly, at 18.34 GMT on 29 June 1985, after covering over 3,000 miles of ocean at an average speed of over 37 knots.

Ball kicking

On 17 February 1974, Robert Smith, 23, of South Cave, East Yorkshire, kicked a standard leather match play football 212 ft from a spot kick to first bounce.

Roger de Villiers, 19, kicked a standard leather match play rugby ball 220 ft from a place kick to first bounce on 18 February 1967 at King Edward VII College Playing Fields, London.

NB. Neither of the above records were wind assisted.

Baseball

The greatest number of 'home runs' hit in a one hour period is 125. The man responsible was the irrepressible George Herman 'Babe' Ruth. As a warm up at Wrigley Field in Los Angeles, USA, in 1927, he was served by six different pitchers, hitting home runs at the rate of approximately one every 30 seconds.

The oldest person still regularly playing baseball is 74-year-old pensioner John Bennett of Southport, Lancashire. John's only complaint is that he's not as quick off the mark as he used to be.

Basketball

On 25 June 1977 at Jacksonville, Florida, USA, Ted St Martin demonstrated the most accurate shooting display ever seen by netting 2,036 consecutive throws from the free spot.

The longest recorded field goal is an estimated 92 ft 6 in (taken from live video recordings) by Bruce Morris of Marshall University in a match against Appalachian State University at Huntingdon, West Virginia, USA, on 8 February 1985.

The longest recorded basketball marathon was completed on 17 April 1983 at Indiana University, Pennsylvania, USA, by two teams from the Sigma Mu fraternity after 102 hours play.

Bicycle race

The most protracted non-mechanical sporting event was the 1926 Tour de France covering 3,569 miles and lasting 29 days.

Bicycle speed record

On 20 July 1985, former US Olympic cycle champion, John Howard, attained a speed of 152 mph, pedalling in the slip stream of a racing saloon car at Bonneville Salt Flats, Utah, USA.

Billiards – amateur

Playing with recognised opponents the following world records are currently claimed:

BEST AVERAGE
(on successive visits to the table):
Two hours: 129.9 by R. Marshall (Australia)
Four hours: 79.9 by L. Driffield (England)

BEST AGGREGATE
Two hours: 1,688 by M. Ferreira (India)
Four hours: 3,202 by M. Ferreira (India)

MOST CENTURIES
Two hours: 10 by M. Ferreira (India)
Four hours: 16 by M. Ferreira (India)

Billiards – professional

In 1930 the Australian, Walter Lindrum, by common consent the greatest ever billiard player, recorded an average of infinity by playing right through one two-hour session, scoring 2,664, which is also the professional session aggregate record. Lindrum also averaged 262 for a fortnight's match, twice made breaks exceeding 3,000 in consecutive visits and made a break of 100 in 46 seconds and 1,011 in 30 minutes.

Canoeing

The fastest recorded time taken to perform 1,000 Eskimo rolls is 44 min 7 sec by Steve Flint at Larkfield Leisure Centre, Maidstone, Kent, on 18 July 1985. At the same venue, Mick Wynne abandoned his paddle and performed 100 hand rolls in 2 min 55.5 sec.

On 13 January 1983, six members of the combined Frome Canoe Club and Frome Caving Group in Somerset completed a unique journey. They paddled a kayak a distance of 3,000 feet through the tortuous caves and passages 400 feet below the Mendip Hills.

Climbing – in a wheelchair

Disabled sportsman Ian Thompson became the first man to reach the summit of the 3,210 feet high Scafell Pike in the Lake District in a wheelchair on 26 August 1986.

Clog skidding

When Arto Neikquist goes bike riding he really gives it some clog! At Santa Pod Raceway, Northampton, riding a 1300 cc Kawasaki motor bike on 17 July 1984, Arto demonstrated his unique ability to slip backwards off the bike and, by holding on to the pillion carrier, be towed along for a mile on his clogs at speeds reaching 120 mph. He then leapt back on to the bike to perform a wheelie, smashing his back light.

Cricket

According to reliable information, the world's oldest cricketer was William Adlam. One summer's afternoon at Taunton, Somerset, in 1888, he shuffled to the wicket at the ludicrous age of 104. Sadly this one brief innings from the tail end of his life is all we know of him, the first 103 years of his cricketing career having passed without comment or note.

The oldest umpire ever to officiate at a first class cricket match was Joseph Fillison (1862–1964) who at the age of 100 umpired the match between Old England and The Lord's Taverners on 19 August 1962.

Croquet

The longest croquet match ever recorded is one of 113 hr 25 min by Hilary Lund-Yates, Hilary Cuthbert, Simon Clay and Roger Swift at

Birmingham University between 18 and 23 June 1983.

Cucumber throwing

On 14 August 1977, Jenny Render of Scunthorpe, Humberside, registered a throw of 102 ft 6 in to become Ladies' British Champion. What ever happened to the men's champion? Answers on a post card please to . . .

Curling

The recent upsurge in the traditionally Celtic sport of curling has brought to light a claim for the marathon record. On 14 to 16 May 1983 at the Capital Water Club, Fredericton, New Brunswick, Canada, Eddie Thomas and John Kohler played continuously for 39 hr 30 min.

Fishing – largest catch

The record for the largest catch ever netted goes to trawler skipper Shaun O'Reily whose small fishing boat, 'Dianti', landed a 3,900 tonne nuclear submarine in the Irish Sea on 7 March 1987.

Floating

The Royal Lifesaving Society recognises three floating positions; the vertical, the

horizontal, and the angle. The duration record for the vertical floating position is held by Les Stewart of Mudjimba, Queensland, Australia, who on 2 February 1982 at the Cotton Tree Swimming Pool, Maroochydore, Queensland, remained in that position for five hours exactly.

Golf

During the qualifying round of the Shawnee invitational for Ladies at Shawnee in Delaware, Pennsylvania, USA, on 21 May 1912, Mrs Maud McInnis took 166 shots to complete the 130 yd par 4 16th hole.

At the par 72 Gott's Park Municipal Course, Leeds, West Yorkshire, on 24 March 1976, David Armitage 'threw' a round of golf on all 18 holes in 3 hr 42 min. David's score of 122 for the round was 50 over par.

Douglas Ferguson was unable to play his usual weekend round of golf at Perranporth, Cornwall, because of a broken arm. Undeterred, he proceeded to play a unique round using his feet, kicking the ball as he went. Douglas took 228 'kick strokes' to return 158 over par for the 18 hole course.

The longest drive of a golf ball over level ground was achieved by Lian Higgins at Baldonnel Airport, Dublin, Eire, on 20 September 1984. The composition of the runway obviously enhanced the ball's bounce as it came to rest, 634 yd 1 in from the tee.

Hang gliding

On 22 May 1984, Rory McCarthy, 23, from London, pushed silently away from a hot air balloon over Hethel airfield, Norfolk, at a height of 35,000 ft. This was the greatest height from which a controlled descent in a hang glider has ever been made.

The oldest person to complete a 20 minute trip in a hang glider, soaring to 500 ft at times, is great-grandmother Martha Morgan, aged 89, of Witney, Oxfordshire. Accompanied by instructor Steve Morris, she completed her feat on 3 July 1984.

High jump – one-legged

The greatest height ever cleared by a one-legged high jumper is 6 ft 8 in by 23-year-old Canadian Arnie Boldt on 3 April 1981 in Rome, Italy.

Hockey marathon

The most protracted game of hockey ever played was one between two teams from Maidstone Hockey Club, Kent, lasting 40 hours from 3 to 4 May 1986.

Human Grand National

The fastest recorded time in which a human has covered the entire Grand National course (without the aid of a horse) at Aintree is 40 min exactly. This was achieved by Peter Regan, headmaster of St Michael's Junior

School, Kirkby, Merseyside, on 10 April 1983. By doing so, he raised more than £6,000 for school funds.

Jogging

The world jogging record was shattered on 31 October 1983, by 40-year-old Australian bread salesman, Ron Grant, when he completed his 10,364 mile round Australia run. Jogging up to 56 miles a day, Ron took 217 days to complete the journey, wearing out 14 pairs of shoes.

Jumping Jacks

The British and European record for Jumping Jacks is 25,450 in 9 hr 30 min, by Colin Hewick of Hull, Humberside. Done in sets of 100 with a 30 second rest between sets, Colin achieved the record at Bishop Burton College of Agriculture, Humberside, on 29 September 1985.

Lakes, meres & waters run

Leaving Loweswater, Cumbria, at 5 am on 25 June 1983, 48-year-old Joss Naylor completed the 106 mile route around the Lake District in the record time of 19 hr 14 min 25 sec.

The undulating route took Joss up ascents totalling 18,000 ft and he dipped his hand in all 27 lakes, meres and waters.

Joss also holds the record for the fastest ascent and descent of the 'Lakelands 72 peaks'. Between 22 and 23 June 1975, he completed the 105 mile course in 23 hr 11 min.

On 5 July 1986, Joss, from Wasdale, Cumbria, added a new record to his tally by climbing all 214 peaks in the Lake District in just 168 hours.

Lawn-mower racing

Lawn-mower racing is fast becoming Britain's most exciting alternative form of motor sport. Speeds of 70 mph are easily attainable from the Group-3 machines.

The longest distance ever travelled by a lawn mower in a 24 hour 'Le Mans' style race is 276 miles by a Temple Tiller Group-3 machine driven variously by Stirling Moss, C. Hartley and Derek Bell at Wisborough Green, West Sussex, between 21 and 22 August 1980.

Leapfrogging

On 19 July 1974, Mike Barwell and Wally Adams, both from East Yorkshire, leapfrogged a distance of 17 miles 342 yards in the permitted eight hour period, averaging one leap every five yards along the disused railway line between Sutton and Hornsea, Humberside.

Parachuting

The first people to parachute off the 984 ft Eiffel Tower were sweethearts Amanda Tucker and Mike McCarthy, both 23, of Yarpole, Herefordshire, on 18 April 1984.

On 2 September 1984, Frenchman Pierre Geveaux became the first man to parachute from the summit of the 14,688 ft Matterhorn mountain.

The greatest number of sky-divers to link arms in a 'star formation' for the mandatory minimum five seconds, is 100 at the National sky-diving championships at Muskogee, Oklahoma, USA, on 5 July 1986.

On 12 September 1986, The Royal Marines freefall parachute team, using military parachutes, claimed a new world record when six members linked up into a stack. Unfortunately the weather stole a little of the glory, as a freak wind necessitated a soggy landing in Southampton Water.

Parachuting – without a chute

In the spring of 1984, 28-year-old American Jim Tyler jumped out of an aeroplane at 10,000 ft without a parachute. Just three seconds earlier Jim had pushed out of the plane a 60 quart baking pot weighted with 20 lb of lead, which contained his parachute. He had just 60 seconds to catch up with the pot, remove the parachute and attach it to his harness. Jim took a little over 53 seconds to achieve his goal, opened the chute and glided safely to the ground.

Dennis Goebel, American stuntman and escapologist was locked into a pair of regulation police handcuffs with chains and manacles fastened to his neck, arms and legs on 17 April 1984, 12,500 ft above the Californian desert. Strapped to his back was a parachute. Dennis was then bundled into an office safe, the door was immediately locked and the safe was pushed out of the plane. Twenty-nine seconds later the safe door burst open. Dennis scrambled out and parachuted to safety.

Parascending

The fastest recorded time for completing the three mile course – swooping under all seven bridges – between Lambeth Bridge and Tower Bridge on the River Thames, is 26 minutes exactly, set on 19 July 1983. The record was set by PC Gil Boyd, 32, and PC Bob Reynolds, 44. The sponsored event raised in excess of £3,000 for the Great Ormond Street Children's Hospital, London, where PC Boyd's son was once a patient.

Seventy-three-year-old George Wheatcroft of Bridlington, Yorkshire, claims to be the world's oldest parascender. On 14 August 1984, he was whisked on a ten minute flight across Bridlington Bay to raise money for his local Round Table.

Peak climbing

On 15 February 1985, Craig Caldwell, 26, of Milngavie, Glasgow, set off on a journey which would involve the climbing of every one of Scotland's Peaks over 2,500 ft – all 499 of them!

Craig finally completed his task on 27 February 1986 on the summit of Ben Lomond, after climbs equivalent to 50 ascents of Mount Everest. Just to travel between climbs involved cycling 2,500 miles and walking a further 3,000 miles.

Press ups

It seems there are no end of ways to perform the perfunctory press up. Listed below are the ones we have ratified claims for. Can you think of any other ways?

FLAT PALMS
29,601 by John Atherton at HMP Featherstone, Yorkshire, between 11 and 12 July 1986. These were performed in sets of 20 with a 30 second rest in between.

ONE ARM
3,836 in four hours by Colin Hewick of Hull at Bodyworld Health Club, Hull, Humberside, on 13 June 1986. These were performed in sets of 25 with a 30 second break in between.

FINGER TIPS
4,674 by Colin Hewick in five hours at Bodyworld Health Club, Hull, Humberside, on 27 February 1987, performed in sets of 25 with a 30 second break in between.

ONE FINGER
45 consecutively by Mick Gooch of Chatham, Kent, on 26 May 1984 at Crystal Palace, London.

ONE THUMB
10 consecutively by Mick Gooch on 1 October 1981 at the Martial Arts Centre, Bristol.

TWO THUMBS
33 consecutively by Mick Gooch on 10 October 1981 at the Martial Arts Centre, Bristol.

BACKS OF HANDS
62 consecutively by Daryl Allen of Durban, South Africa, on 29 September 1986.

ONE FINGER ON A COCONUT
16 consecutively by Mick Gooch on TV AM's 'Wide Awake Club' on 12 January 1985.

ONE FINGER ON A BEER CAN
10 consecutively (yes, it was the beer that refreshes parts that other beers can't reach!) by Mick Gooch at The Bull Inn, Maidstone, Kent on 16 December 1984.

MOST IN FIVE MINUTES
294 by Colin Hewick at Jackson's Club, Hull, Humberside, on 14 October 1981.

Racing pigeons

The most unsuccessful pigeon race ever held was started on 16 August 1978 at Preston, Lancashire, with the release of 6,745 birds, in ideal weather conditions. Twenty-four hours later only 1,200 birds were accounted for; the rest simply vanished, never to be heard of again.

On 29 June 1953, 'Blue Lady' was released by her owner Harry Town at

Neyland, Pembrokeshire, for a leisurely flight home to her loft in Carmarthen (about 30 miles). Eleven years later she was returned by a fancier in Brazil, by post, dead, in a cardboard box!

Roller limbo

Since its inauguration in 1981, the roller limbo record appears to be stuck at the height of five inches. Joint world record holders are now Denise Culp of Rock Hill, South Carolina, USA, and Tracey O'Callaghan and Sandra Siviour, both of Bexley North, NSW, Australia.

Rowing the Thames

Dean Bird, Steve Debenham, Mathew Hardy, Robert Stevens and Keith Vegg, all firemen from Poplar, East London, made up the team which gained the world record for the fastest row of the River Thames. Starting at Lechlade Bridge, Gloucestershire, at 9 am on 16 April 1984, they completed their voyage at Southend Pier, Essex, 45 hr 32 min later, at 6.32 am on 18 April 1984, having rowed a distance of 185.66 miles.

Running

The first relay team to complete the 1,680 miles round trip from Land's End to John O'Groats and back again non-stop consisted of 10 members of the Royal Horse Artillery Regiment. The feat took exactly one week to complete, ending on 25 August 1983.

Probably the most gruelling of all long distance runs is the six day event. The longest distance achieved over six consecutive days is 614 miles by Yiannis Kouros of Greece at a meeting in Colac, Victoria, Australia, between 26 November and 1 December 1984.

The female record stands at 484 miles, set at the same event by 37-year-old Nottingham housewife Eleanor Adams. The fastest recorded time taken to run 1,000 miles is 12 days 12 hr 36 min 20 sec by Siegfried Bauer of New Zealand between 15 and 28 November 1983 in a road race continually encircling Melbourne and Colac, Victoria, Australia.

Running backwards

The longest distance achieved by running backwards for seven consecutive days is 340 miles by Walter Cornelius of Peterborough between 14 and 20 April 1959.

Running – custard-filled wellies

The great custard-filled welly extravaganza continues! On 31 August 1986, at 'The Alternative Olympics' held at the Costello International Sports Stadium, Hull, Humberside, Patrick Howson of Brentwood, Essex, ran 100 metres in custard-filled wellies in the record time of 13.82 seconds.

The fastest female in custard-filled wellies over 100 metres is Sally Lowe of Hassocks, West Sussex, with a time of 16.01 seconds.

At the same meeting, Gary Spring of Brentwood, Essex, broke his own one mile in custard-filled wellies record, with a time of 5 min 21.37 sec.

Also recorded was the fastest time for a Veteran (over 50) by Derek Earl, 52, of Hassocks, West Sussex, with a time of 5 min 27.89 sec.

The fastest female over a mile in custard-filled wellies is Barbara Rickard of Ditching, West Sussex, who performed the feat at Adastra Park, Hassocks, West Sussex, on 1 September 1984 with a time of 8 min 14.80 sec.

On 17 May 1986, 'The Brentwood Police & Gateway International Custard-Filled Welly Challengers', consisting of 27 sticky legged individuals, successfully completed a 26 mile 385 yards relay marathon in the record time of 3 hr 3 min 26.6 sec at Shenfield School, Shenfield, Essex.

Not to be outdone, the ladies came along and triumphed also, recording a

world beating time of 4 hr 50 min 16.41 sec for the same distance.

Shooting

In the harsh winter of 1962, on 10 January, Major A. J. Coates shot and killed a record bag of 550 wood pigeons in six hours near his home at Winchester, Hampshire.

Shot putting

Ambidextrous shot putter Allan Feuerbach holds the world record for consecutive shot putts with different hands. At Malmö, Sweden, on 24 August 1974, Allan's putts totalled 121 ft 6¾ in. The right hand putt measured 70 ft 1¾ in and the left hand 51 ft 5 in.

Sit ups

Chris Howson, aged 27, from Darwen, Lancashire, set a new world record on 15 November 1982 by performing 112 sit ups in two minutes.

The female record is held by Lorraine Foster of Scunthorpe, Humberside, with a total of 110 sit ups in two minutes on 17 July 1983.

Skateboarding

Trevor Baxter, 19, gained the world high jump record of 5 ft 5.7 in on 14 September 1982 at Grenoble, France.

In clearing 17 barrels, Tony Alva, 19, created a new world skateboarding long jump record of 17 ft 5 in at the 4th US Skateboard Association Championships at Signal Hill, California, on 25 September 1977.

Skiing

On 15 February 1984 at Montreal, Canada, a unique 'hot dogging' backwards somersault was performed simultaneously by 28 people all linking hands.

The most stylish and rigorous ascent and descent from 14,000 ft of Mont Blanc took place in the summer of 1931, when Alfred C. Tartuffe took exactly 11 hours to complete the route from base to summit and back. He departed after a hot croissant breakfast, got to the summit in time for a pâté lunch and arrived back down again in time to dress for dinner.

French stuntman René Retez holds the world record for skiing through a tunnel of fire. At Alvar in the French Alps, in front of a crowd of 3,000 people in the spring of 1983, René took only eight seconds to complete the 80 yard downhill course.

The 24 hour ski endurance record is held by Teuvo Rantanen, who between 4 and 5 March 1984 covered 190 miles at Jyvaskyla, Finland.

Skipping

The greatest number of turns of a skipping rope executed in 10 seconds is 128 by Albert Naylor at Stanford Sports Stadium, Birmingham, on 19 November

1982. At Lydd Airport on 25 September 1985, Albert performed approximately 420 turns in one minute. Although a video was taken by Fuji TV of Japan, it could not be given total definition to confirm this as a new world record.

Walter Cornelius skipped continuously for 90 minutes using a 48 lb link of chain at the Municipal Swimming Baths, Peterborough, on 22 August 1969.

Snooker

The longest marathon on record was completed on 26 May 1985 after 300 hours play by Sam Ellis and Glyn Travis at the Bridlington Snooker Centre, Humberside. The event raised over £2,000 for the David Pinder Liver Transplant Fund.

The highest possible break at snooker is not, as commonly believed, 147. By adhering rigorously to the rules a break of 155 is possible. In order for this to happen one player must play a foul stroke and render his opponent snookered. The referee will then call a 'free ball' and the snookered player may now attempt to pot ANY ball on the table. If potted, this ball has the value of a red (one point) and is re-spotted; then the player may continue with a colour. Thus by sequence a break of 155 is possible. It was reported in March 1980 that Alex 'Hurricane' Higgins had achieved a break of 154 in just such a fashion.

The fastest recorded time that a frame of snooker has been completed using a potato as the cue ball is 1 hr 13 min by Gary Milner and Stuart Allerston on 4 February 1983 at the Birkholme Country Club, Hedon, North Humberside.

Soccer

The soccer match with the unenviable record of attracting the lowest crowd ever was one staged between Leicester City and Stockport County on 7 May 1921. Stockport should have been the home venue, but at the last minute the FA invoked a suspension rule due to the crumbling terraces. A hasty phone call was made to the Old Trafford ground of Manchester United and an agreement made that the match would take place there. Official gate figures showed a paying audience of 13, although it is believed many more entered free at half-time.

The only animal – human or otherwise – known to have drowned in the players' bath, was the local mascot of Greenock Morton FC (now just Morton) in the season of 1910–11. Centre forward Tom Gracie was given a sheep named Toby in appreciation for his goal scoring prowess, which became the club mascot. Unfortunately, Toby was left one day in the players' changing rooms whilst the team celebrated victory in a local pub. When Tom returned he found Toby drowned in the players' bath.

Sporting record breaker

Between 24 January 1970 and 1 November 1977 Russian weightlifter Vasili Alexeyev broke 80 official world records for weightlifting.

Standing jumps

Ray Ewry holds the following world records for various jumps from a standing start:

High Jump: 5 ft 5 ins
Long Jump: 11 ft 4 in
Triple Jump: 22 ft 3 in
Backwards Long Jump: 9 ft 3 in

All these records were set at the three Olympic Games between 1900 and 1908.

Stationary cycling

On 1 October 1959, Rudi Jan Josef de Greef stood motionless on a bike for the record time of 10 hours at Malaga, Spain.

Swimming

The first swimmer to cross Loch Ness and back, non-stop, was 19-year-old David Morgan from Scarborough, North Yorkshire. David completed the 47 mile swim in 23 hr 5 min between 26 and 27 August 1983.

David Morgan also holds the record for the fastest one way crossing of Loch Ness, with a time of 9 hr 57 min on 31 July 1983.

On 13 July 1983, 'Oh Calcutta' actress Julie Ridge, 26, became the first person to swim non-stop around Manhattan Island, New York, in a time of 21 hr 30 min. The only difficulty Julie encountered was avoiding the abundance of human effluent in the river.

The greatest distance ever swum underwater (without the aid of hyperventilating equipment) is 165 yards by Walter Cornelius at the Municipal Swimming Baths, Peterborough, on 17 September 1970.

Tandem walkers

Denise Mitchell, 14, balanced herself atop the feet of Dave Wallbank, 22, and together they walked tandem fashion for a distance of four miles between Llanwrda and Llandovery, Dyfed, Wales, on 26 March 1975.

Tiddlywinks

On BBC TV's 'Blue Peter' programme on 24 April 1986, four members of the English Tiddlywink Association all cleared the bar set at 7 ft 6 in to claim a new tiddlywink high jump record.

The longest recorded marathon by a team of six is 300 hours by the Southampton University Tiddlywink Club between 20 February and 5 March 1981.

Trimball

Start a new craze and somebody will claim a world record for doing something with it.

At the first 'Disk-O-Hopper' (Trimball) championship held at Northampton on 4 October 1986, 11-year-old James Carroll of Kingsthorpe, Northants, set a new world record of 22,810 bounces non-stop in two hours.

Tug of war

On 12 August 1889 at Jubbulpore, India, two companies of the 2nd Battalion of the Derbyshire Regiment staged what was probably the world's most tedious sporting event. So well matched were they in muscle and lack of guile that their tug of war contest lasted no less than 2 hr 41 min. During this absurd length of time, the winning team, 'H' Company, moved a net distance of only four yards, giving them an average speed of just 0.00084 mph.

Underground walking

The greatest depth at which a 26 mile 385 yard marathon has been walked is 3,000 ft at Florence Colliery, Stoke on Trent, by four miners; so raising £1,400 for local charities.

Underwater bike riding

The greatest distance achieved in an underwater bike riding marathon is 87.81 miles by a team of 32 in 72 hours at Norvik, Norway, between 28 and 31 March 1984.

A team of 32 'swim cyclers' from Tuscon, Arizona, USA, completed a 60 hour marathon relay on a special weighted tricycle at the Amphi High School pool between 27 and 29 November 1981. They covered a record distance of 64.96 miles.

At Sheffield swimming baths on 20 November 1982, a team of four 'swim cyclers' wearing scuba gear on specially weighted bikes completed an underwater relay race (each member completing one 33 metre length) in 4 mins 16.5 sec.

Walking

At Moor Park, Preston, Lancashire, between 29 April and 5 May 1986, Tom Benson, 53, walked non-stop for 6 days 12 hours 45 minutes covering a total distance of 415 miles.

The greatest distance achieved in 24 hours is 140 miles by Paul Forthomme at Woluwé, Belgium, on 14 October 1984.

The shortest time taken to walk the 885 miles between Land's End and John O'Groat's is 12 days 3 hours 45 minutes achieved by Malcolm Barnish between 9 and 21 June 1986.

The only claimant for multiple walkings twixt John O'Groat's and Land's End is Bob Thornton of Almondsbury, Bristol, Avon, who since 1972 has completed the journey three times, raising thousands of pounds for the National Star Centre of Disabled Youth at Cheltenham. Bob is the founder member of the Jogle Club, for those who have similarly walked the route, and would like to hear from others who wish to join.

The fastest recorded time taken to walk 1,000 miles is 15 days 23 hours 58 minutes by 54-year-old John Dowling of Sheffield, Yorkshire, ending on 20 March 1984.

The greatest distance achieved whilst walking backwards in 24 hours is 84 miles by Tony Thornton at Minneapolis, Massachusetts, USA, on 1 January 1986.

Walking on hands

The greatest distance ever covered in eight days whilst walking on hands is 153 miles by Walter Cornelius from Cambridge to London and back between 2 and 9 April 1968.

The only known exponent of the art of walking backwards on hands is Raymond Knopfler of Norfolk, Virginia. It was reported that on 17 February 1975, Raymond walked backwards on his hands along Main Street – a distance of 400 yards – in exactly 30 minutes.

Water skiing

The greatest number of water skiers towed simultaneously behind a 65 ft power boat for a distance of one mile is 80, achieved by members of the Powerboat and Ski Club, Cairns, Australia, on 24 August 1985.

The youngest person ever to achieve the distinction of being able to water ski and remain on course for at least 100 yards was six month old Parks Bonifay. At the age of only three days Parks began his basic training assisted by his father Peter. His record breaking run was performed in July 1982 at Cypress Gardens, Florida, USA.

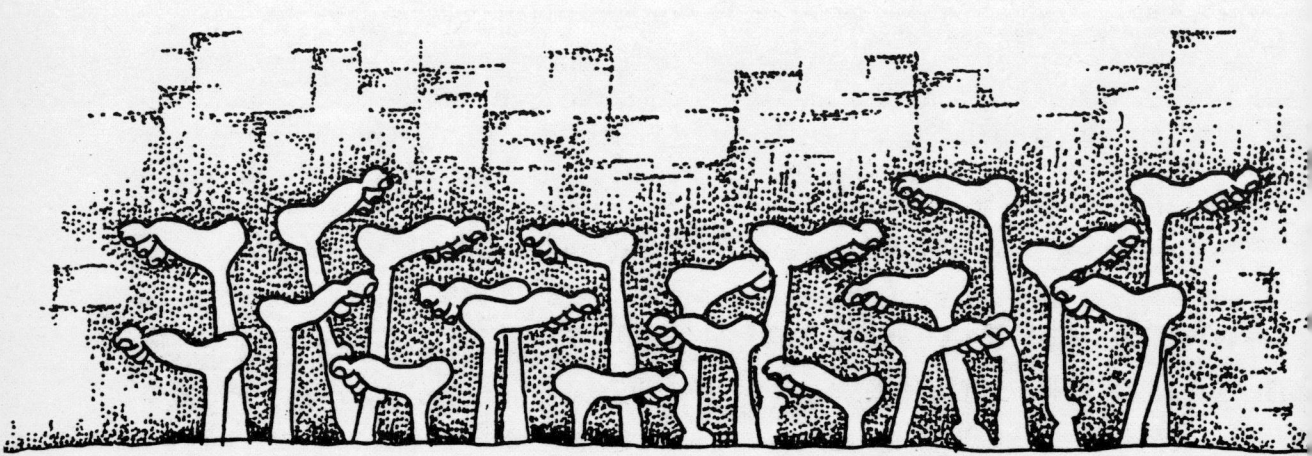

Weightlifting

The greatest number of weightlifting records to be broken in one day at different levels of class is 11 by George McHugh at Wellfield Comprehensive School, Wingate, County Durham on 12 March 1986.

Wheelie on a bike

The longest recorded duration for 'pulling a wheelie' on a bicycle is 1 hr 16 min 54 sec by Craig Strong at Picketts Lock Sports Centre, London, on 7 January 1983.

Wind surfing

The longest distance ever travelled on a wind surfing sail board is 1,794 miles whilst circumnavigating Great Britain by Tim Batston in 39 days between 2 May and 10 July 1984.

With a minimum wind speed of 25 mph, the longest recorded time established for riding a wind surfing practice board is 7 mins 53 sec by Tim Kemp, 20, of Rochester, Kent, on 9 September 1984 at Gravesend, Kent.

The world endurance record for non-stop wind surfing is 90 hr 45 min by Simon Bornhoft, 21, of Havant, Hampshire, ending on 17 August 1986. Simon sailed from Weymouth to Brighton.

Chapter Six

THAT'S ENTERTAINMENT?

Accordion playing

Starting at 12.00 noon on 14 August 1982, Tom Luxton of Oldbury, Warley, West Midlands, played his accordion continuously for a total of 84 hours, ending at 12.00 midnight on Saturday 17 August 1982. Tom's marathon was performed at the Robin Hood pub at Quarry Bank, West Midlands, and raised over £3,000 to buy a heart monitoring machine for Wolverhampton Hospital.

After dinner speaking

The longest after dinner speech ever made was one lasting 24 hr 1 min by Methodist lay preacher Andrew Page, 23, hailing from Woolton, Liverpool. Andrew's speech was performed between 1 and 2 July 1986 at St George's Hotel, Liverpool and 17 fellow diners lasted through the duration.

Bingo

At the Executive Park Bingo Parlour, Michigan, USA, there's only one player who is virtually guaranteed to win every time. That's because Terry Nachutuk regularly plays bingo with 130 cards! The highest number of cards that Terry has played with is 133, with the caller shouting out numbers at the rate of one every two seconds. Oh yes! There's another strange thing about Terry, he doesn't use markers, he just remembers the numbers in his head.

Break dancing

Six youngsters comprising the Breakdance team, 'Street Machine', led by Brian Numan, set a new world record on 3 May 1986 at Salford, Lancashire, by dancing non-stop for 2 hr 45 min.

Busker

Under a little-used British by-law dating back to 1904, 'The World's Worst Busker' – red haired punk Michael Hogg – was fined three pounds for playing a musical instrument less than 100 yards from a shop. The shop manager, Mr David Hamilton-Peskett, called the police after Michael's 'non-political punk music' became a constant source of annoyance to both staff and customers.

Bustiest leading lady

The world's most generously endowed (and proportioned) leading lady was 26-year-old Doris Wishman. Choosing the stage name of 'Chesty Morgan' she paraded her 73 inch bosom as a star of the 1975 epic *Deadly Weapons*.

Cheese

One of the most bizarre exhibits ever to be displayed as a work of art was a smelly 17-year-old Gouda cheese. Taking pride of place at the Barbican Centre, London, during the whole of February 1986, the 10 inch cheese was displayed as part of an exhibition by the German sculptor Dieter Roth. The cheese is owned by the Museum of Modern Art in Vienna. It is bluish-grey in colour and covered with evil smelling mould.

Choirboy

On 19 June 1986, John Love Vokins of Hathersage, Derbyshire, celebrated two anniversaries. It was his 96th birthday, and John maintained his status as the oldest serving choirboy in the world; it also marked his 91st consecutive year as a chorister.

Comic strip

The longest running current comic strip still printed is the 'Katzenjammer Kids'. The adventures of Hans and Fritz first appeared in the New York Journal on 12

December 1897 and are still published in several American periodicals to this day.

Crossword puzzle

The longest time taken to complete *The Times* crossword is 34 years 1 month. On 4 May 1966, *The Times* received a letter from Mrs Mirielle Tréport from the Fiji Isles announcing that she had just completed the crossword in the 4 April 1932 edition. Her mother had started it all those years ago but without success. The newspaper then spent many years living in a trunk in the attic of Mrs Tréport's sister in London. When rediscovered, the puzzle was sent with a host of others to Fiji to the puzzle-mad Mirielle. Years later she finished it and proudly sent the correct solution to *The Times.*

Dancing

The most protracted bout of Belly Dancing ever achieved was a marathon session lasting 106 hours by Eileen Foucher at Rush Green Hospital, Romford, Essex, between 30 July and 3 August 1984.

Director – most prolific

The most prolific film director in the history of the motion picture was Canadian Allan Divan, who directed a total of 407 films between 1909 and 1981.

Disco dancing

The most protracted session of disco dancing ever staged was the 408 hr marathon by Peter Stewart, 25, of Wednesfield, Wolverhampton, between 6 and 21 August 1983 at the Cannon Hill Art Centre, Birmingham.

Peter's marathon world record raised over £2,500 for local hospitals so that an ultra-sonic scalpel could be purchased to save the life of a local schoolgirl.

Drumming

According to reliable information, as yet unconfirmed, Trevor Mitchell of Scunthorpe claimed a new world record of 44 days for non-stop drumming.

Escapology

World famous escapologist Harry Houdini (born 1874 as Ehrich Weiss) performed a unique escape. He was sealed in a metal coffin which was then submerged under water. One hour and 42 seconds later he escaped and surfaced. Experts afterwards stated they had thought him dead, as the volume of air contained in the sealed coffin was only sufficient to sustain life for approximately 15 minutes.

On 9 September 1984 at Gravesend, Kent, Nick Jansen escaped from a pair of regulation police handcuffs in 6.5 seconds. It was Nick's 1,020th consecutive escape.

European lama

From the moment of his birth in Granada State Hospital, Spain, on 12 February 1985, it was suspected that Osel Hita Torres was no ordinary child. That has now been confirmed, for on 12 March 1987 he was enshrined as the first European-born lama, the reincarnation of Lama Thubten Yeshe, who died in 1984, having brought Tibetan Buddhism to the West.

Fastest sell out

The fastest selling concert tickets ever went on sale at 8.30 am on 21 January 1983. By 12.30 pm, 23,820 had been sold for the 12 performances of 'Barry Manilow in Concert' at the Uris Theatre, New York, USA. Sales realised a total of over $782,000.

Film watching

Cinema usherette Jennie Ashton set a new world record on 7 June 1986 for watching boring films after spending 83 hours enduring 58 non-stop screenings of the old Ronald Reagan movie, *Bedtime for Bonzo*. Jennie won £500 and a holiday for two in London.

The runner-up quit after sitting through 61 hours of the 1978 epic *Attack of the Killer Tomatoes*.

Fire-eating

Jean Leggett of Stoke Poges, Buckinghamshire, is the most voracious lady fire-eater the world has ever seen. Jean has travelled the world giving demonstrations of her fire-eating skills and just for kicks she sometimes does it blindfolded! Jean's current world fire-eating records are:

1. 6,607 flames in two hours
2. 174 flames in two minutes
3. 74 flames in one minute
4. Holding a burning torch in her teeth for 19 seconds

Gladiator

The most successful gladiator the world has ever seen was Commodus Lucius Aelius Aurelius (AD 161–192). During the latter part of his short life he became Emperor of Rome, but still continued to fight in the arena, having 1,031 successful combats before being strangled to death by a wrestler named Narcissus.

Handbell ringing

The longest continuous handbell ringing concert ever performed was one lasting 56 hours by 12 pupils from Ecclesfield School, Sheffield, Yorkshire, from 21 to 23 July 1985.

Head in a rat cage

Dave Wakefield, assistant to the famous Ken Edwards (the 'Ratman and Robin' duo) endured a time of 9 min 45 sec with his head in a 12 in × 12 in × 18 in wire cage filled with 12 wild rats at 'The Alternative Olympics', Hull, Humberside, on 31 August 1986.

High diving fireball

Fifty-six-year-old stunt driver Don Lindberg regularly dives from a 60 ft tower with his petrol-soaked clothes alight, into a six feet deep tank of water which in turn is ablaze. After years of perfection, Don's stunt won him a world title in the High Diving Championships at Leeds, Yorkshire, in August 1984.

High diving mules

Currently on tour throughout the USA are 'Tim Rivers Original High Diving Aqua Mules'. The Mules, who according to Mr Rivers 'love their work', jump from platforms of varying heights into a large tank of water. The grand finale is a leap from 30 ft – the highest ever attained.

Hole – most expensive

German experimental artist Joseph Beuys drilled a hole in the wall of Dusseldorf Art Gallery and declared it a 'work of art'. His masterpiece was valued by experts and insured for £10,000.

Human regurgitation

The world's only acknowledged human regurgitator is Scotsman Stevie Starr. Stevie is able to 'bring back' swallowed objects on command and in the case of multiple swallowings, he can regurgitate objects in any order requested. Stevie practised and perfected his unusual act during his upbringing in an orphanage, where he conceived the idea that the safest place to keep his pocket money was in his stomach.

Juggling

In the 1985 World Circus Championships in London, American Dick Franco demonstrated his unique ability to juggle six ping pong balls with his mouth. Dick is also the only man ever to master the art of juggling three working chainsaws.

Alexander Poskitt (d. 1985) of Newtown, Powys, Wales, was the only person ever able to juggle five live hedgehogs with ungloved hands.

According to reliable information, the only man in history able to juggle (as opposed to 'shower') ten balls at a time was the Italian, Enrico Rastelli, during his 20 year career, which sadly ended in 1931.

Longest film

The longest film ever shown was one entitled, *The Longest and Most*

Meaningless Movie in the World, lasting exactly 48 hours.

Manuscripts – most rejected

As most would-be authors know, it is a tremendous task having your manuscripts accepted by a publisher. Nevertheless, take a leaf from Mr Gilbert Young's book and keep trying. Since 1958, Mr Young has submitted the manuscript of his book, *World Government Crusade*, to no less than 106 different publishers throughout the world. Each time it was returned with a rejection slip. Mr Young reviews his potential bestseller as 'a policy for the establishment of one government for the whole world, with one police force and one compulsory language'.

Memory man

The world's number one memory man is American Harry Lorraine. His stage and cabaret shows are a sellout throughout the world as he constantly amazes his audiences with his tremendous memory capacity. At a recent show in New York, USA, Harry was introduced to a section of the audience – 118 individuals. One hour later he was able to identify without error every single individual by name.

Creighton Carvello has recently started to cash in on his amazing memory by giving demonstrations on the club circuit. Teesider Creighton's main claim to fame is his ability to recite the definition 'pi' to more than 20,000 decimal places.

He also holds the world record for recalling the sequence of 308 playing cards after sighting them only once at the New Marske Institute Club, Middlesbrough, on 21 March 1985.

Creighton's other feats of memory power include being able to recall the names of every footballer who has played in an FA Cup final; the telephone numbers of all 92 English Football League clubs; every Derby and Grand National winner with weights, jockeys and prices; every number one record plus date it reached that position.

Morris dancing – across bridges

The Earl of Stamford's Morris Side, based in Wilmslow, Cheshire, created a new record on Saturday 16 November 1985, by dancing across Britain's three longest suspension bridges (the Forth, the Humber and Severn) in 22 hr 15 min. The total distance covered was 896 miles.

One-legged bicycle diving

The greatest height from which a one-legged (or two-legged for that matter) person has dived, remaining seated and upright on a bicycle until 'splash down' is 95 feet.

In 1902, a 23-year-old American simply called Mr Gifford performed this feat twice daily at the London Hippodrome, diving from a platform under the roof into the flooded arena.

One song marathon

For 63 hours ending on 25 August 1983, the American radio station KFJCFM in Berkeley, California, continually broadcast the 21-year-old rock 'n' roll number, 'Louie Louie'.

Some 800 different renderings were broadcast, most of them the painful offerings of the station's listeners. The lesser-known performances included 'The Bowl of Slugs' and 'Little Nymph and the Spectonettes'.

Organ playing – with a difference!

Multi-talented organist Adrian Wigley, 41, of Brownhills, West Midlands, plays the organ the hard way; with his nose and tongue.

On 31 October 1985 at the Railway Tavern, Brownhills, he played tunes on the organ using only his tongue for a record two hours non-stop.

On 23 July 1985 at The Traveller's Rest, Burntwood, West Midlands, Adrian completed a six hour non-stop organ playing marathon with his nose.

Organ recital

The longest recital ever performed on an electric organ was one lasting 411 hours by Scunthorpe drag artist Vince 'Vanessa' Bull at The Comet Hotel, Scunthorpe, Humberside, from 2 to 19 June 1977.

The longest recital ever performed on a church organ was one lasting 110 hours by Angie Thompson at St Stephen's Church, Newport, Humberside, between 16 and 20 April 1985.

Pantomine cow

At 'The Alternative Olympics', Hull, on 31 August 1986, Kevin Harris (front) and Phil Clark (rear) set a new world record for the one mile pantomine cow race with a time of 7 min 59.01 sec.

At Fosters' Festival of Records, Gravesend, Kent, on 9 September 1984, a new world record for the pantomine cow 50 metres dash was set at 9.97 seconds by Keith Martin (front) and Janet Pinder (rear).

Piano playing – upside down

Club pianist and entertainer Colin 'Fingers' Henry is so versatile he literally plays the piano standing on his head.

On 22 December 1986 at Teddy's Club, Withernsea, Humberside, Colin set a new duration record by playing the piano standing on his head for 1 min 29.43 sec.

Quick time musician

On 28 May 1985, it was reported that Rory Blackwell, 51, recorded the fastest ever rendition of 'When the Saints Go Marching In', by playing 314 different instruments in just 84 seconds. The former 'Beach Boys' drummer set the record at a holiday camp in Dawlish, Devon.

Quiz show prize

Computer expert Michael Dixon of Marford, Wrexham, Clwyd, won the biggest cash prize ever awarded on a British TV Quiz Show when scooping £7,455 on ITV's 'Winner Takes All', screened on 18 July 1986.

Radio broadcast – longest

The longest recorded radio broadcast was achieved by Larry Norton of WGRQ Radio, Buffalo, New York, USA, between 19 March and 8 April 1981 – a total of 484 hours.

Radio phone-in

Max Nottingham of Lincoln claims to hold the world record for the most number of successful calls to radio phone-ins. During 1985 he chatted and aired his views 272 times on 12 different stations.

Rats in tights

Ratcatcher Ken Edwards and his assistant regularly perform with live wild rats. Catching them in the sewers of Manchester, Ken cleans them up in his bath before stuffing them down the front of the fishnet tights he wears during his stage act. The record number of wild rats Ken has stuffed down his tights is 47.

Record – fastest selling

Issued on that fateful date of 22 November 1963, the LP record 'John Fitzgerald Kennedy – A Memorial Album' sold 4,000,000 copies in just six days.

Record recognition

Still the only person to demonstrate the amazing ability to correctly identify the title of a classical hi-fi record by merely looking at the groove pattern is Doctor Arthur Lintgen of Pennsylvania, USA. On some of the more popular records, Arthur Lintgen can even name the orchestra, the conductor and at which studio it was recorded.

Arthur would have little difficulty in guessing the title of one particular record: its size would give it away. The smallest gramophone record ever made was a $1\frac{3}{8}$ inch diameter recording of 'God Save the King' by the HMV Record Company in 1924. Only 250 were ever produced.

Rope tricks

The only man to demonstrate the amazing ability to spin 12 ropes simultaneously was the American Roy Vincent, in a 20 year career from 1933 to 1953.

Shooting

Whilst touring Germany with her rodeo in the early part of this century, legendary markswoman Annie Oakley was challenged by Crown Prince William to shoot off the end of a cigarette held between his lips. Not wanting to shoot too close to the royal face, Annie obliged by just shooting away the ash leaving the cigarette still alight. She did this from a standing position at a distance of 100 feet.

Singing

The longest singing marathon ever recorded is one of 180 hours by Robert Sim at The Waterfront Hotel, Hull, Humberside, between 18 and 25 March 1983.

Sketch – most expensive

On 8 November 1986 at Sotheby's auction house, London, a record $3,630,000 was paid by an anonymous American collector for a small two-sided sketch by Leonardo da Vinci.

Stage performance

Joseph Pujol – 'Le Petomane' – entertained millions at the famous Moulin Rouge, Paris, between 1892 and 1900 by passing wind in a variety of musical notes, playing tunes which included a rendering of the French National Anthem. In addition, again using only 'wind power', Pujol could blow out a candle at a distance of half a metre. At private functions, completely naked, he would plunge his bottom into a large container of water and using his sphincter muscles he would then draw up a great quantity of water through his anus into his large intestine. Removing himself from the container, he would bend over and expel the water with such force that he could knock over skittles at a distance of four metres.

Stunt – most expensive

Joint world record holders for the biggest fee ever paid to a stunt man are Britain's Roy Alon and American's Dar Robinson, who each received a cool one million dollars to perform their stunts.

Dar Robinson made a controlled leap (using cable and ratchet gear) from the CN Tower Toronto (1,100 ft) for the film *High Point*.

Roy Alon fell backwards off a cliff into the sea whilst seated in a wheelchair with one leg in plaster and firing a bazooka for the film *Curse of the Pink Panther*.

TV commercial – least successful

Comedienne Pat Coombes is the proud holder of the record for the greatest number of unsuccessful 'takes' for a TV commercial. In April 1973, whilst making a commercial for a breakfast cereal, she forgot her lines 28 times. The line she forgot on every occasion was the name of the product – a type of muesli. Pat became so nervous and frustrated that the commercial was never finished.

Theatre – world's smallest

It's a fully functioning theatre, conceived on the grand scale, with a conventional stage, a front curtain and an impressive lighting system. The lavish decorations in the auditorium are worthy of the Royal Opera House, Covent Garden. Yet this ornate construction is all mounted on the sidecar of a motor-bike and the audience capacity is two!

The World's Smallest Theatre is owned and run by Marcel Steiner of Surbiton, Surrey, and regularly performs at indoor and outside carnivals and festivals throughout Britain. Among the best remembered performances are:

A four-act dramatisation of Charles Dickens' *A Christmas Carol*, lasting 15 minutes and complete with the Great Blizzard of 1843.

A 10 minute version of Shakespeare's *The Tempest*, performed in the car park of The Royal Shakespeare Theatre, Stratford-upon-Avon.

An epic adaptation of *The Guns of Navarone*, featuring the scaling of the cliffs, the blowing up of the guns and all the significant action from the film.

Tightrope walking

The first crossing of the Niagara Falls on a tightrope was made by Jean Francois Gravelet (Charles Blondin) on 30 June 1859. The rope was 110 feet long and stretched 160 feet above the falls.

The only man able to walk a tightrope whilst attached to two foot wooden stilts is four times world champion Manfred Doval of Germany.

Tower fall

Stunt man and James Bond stand-in Mike Potter holds the world record for a controlled fall from a tower. On 27 May 1983, Mike 'fell' 85 feet from a specially constructed tower on to a landing pad of foam rubber and cardboard boxes measuring 10 ft 6 in square and 7 ft deep.

Tray balancing

On BBC TV's 'Late, Late, Breakfast Show' on 9 January 1986, Abdul Hasani broke his own world record by successfully balancing 205 plastic beakers between 41 layers of trays, then lifting them up with one hand.

Chapter Seven

PUB GAMES AND PASTIMES

Arm wrestling

The most protracted bout of arm wrestling ever recorded was a contest staged on 28 May 1982 at Cockermouth, Cumbria, between Phil Davis and Jack Poulsom, lasting exactly 24 hours.

Bar billiards

In league matches, most games of bar billiards last about 20 minutes before the bar drops and the balls fail to return. The greatest number of points accrued during a game of bar billiards is 28,530 by Keith Sheard at The Crown and Thistle, Headington, Oxford, on 9 July 1984.

The highest score achieved by a team of five over a 24 hour period is 1,506,570 by the team from The Hour Glass, Sands, High Wycombe, Bucks, between 26 and 27 November 1982.

The longest bar billiards marathon ever staged was one lasting 57 hours between 28 February and 2 March 1987 at Tillingbourne Green, Kent. The players were publican Bob Waterton and brewery worker Ian Ladd.

Beer mat flipping

Mention the words 'beer mat' and Felixstowe man Dean Gould will really flip his lid! Dean holds every beer mat flipping record in this category and will readily demonstrate his skills at his local pub, 'The Feathers'.

Standardisation requires that the beer mats be approximately 10 centimetres square. The mats must revolve half a turn after being flipped from the edge of the table before being caught in the same hand with the fingers on top, thumb underneath in a pincer position.

Right Hand Flipping: 90
Left Hand Flipping: 90
Simultaneous Flipping: 130 (65 in each hand)
Speed Flipping: 1,000 in 37 seconds

In addition, Dean set a new world record for beer mat catching on 1 September 1985. At Chantry Fête, Ipswich, Suffolk, he successfully caught 600 beer mats, flipped from the elbows (similar to coin snatching) in one hand, palm uppermost.

Beer mat stuffing

The greatest number of standard beer mats ever stuffed in the mouth and held in the teeth is 76, by Gary (Garfield) Higginson at the Shakespeare Inn, Hedon, Humberside, on 7 January 1986.

Bottle stretching

The longest distance ever stretched to place a half pint beer bottle on the ground is 8 ft 5½ in by Ken Smith at the Jolly Pirate, Falmouth, Cornwall on 20 August 1978.

Chair lifting

Alan Pickering of Darlington, Cleveland, claims he can lift a bar chair weighing 18½ lb to the vertical 25 times in one minute. Alan's records also include 200 lifts in 30 minutes and 310 in one hour.

Coin snatching

As all traditional coin snatchers will know, the coins must be snatched using the 'palm down' technique. The greatest number of ten pence pieces snatched in this fashion is 132 by 22-year-old Dean Gould at The Feathers Pub, Felixstowe, Suffolk, on 6 January 1987.

Cue lifting

Jim Mills lifted 24 16 oz billiard cues simultaneously, holding only the tapered tips, from the vertical to the horizontal (through 90 degrees) at Alfreton Park, Derbyshire, on 13 June 1982.

Jim went on to set a new world record by lifting a 22 oz cue 1,005 times consecutively by the same method.

Darts

Timed high scores:

Twenty-four hours – Team of eight: 1,722,249 by Broken Hill Darts Club, Broken Hill, NSW, Australia, between 28 and 29 September 1985.

Twelve hours – Team of four: 332,986 by regulars at the Lockavullin Bar, Oban, Scotland, on 11 January 1986.

Six hours – Pairs: 179,476 by David Jones and Eddie Norcross at The Junction, East London, on 14 December 1984.

The least number of darts taken to score one million is 37,809 by a team of eight players from the Gardener's Arms, Ipswich, between 28 February and 2 March 1986.

Darts marathon

The longest recorded darts marathon was one of 168 hours by Dave Dingley and Mick Poole at The Three Horse Shoes, Malvern, Worcester, between 16 and 23 November 1986.

Darts — using six-inch nails

We have all heard stories about the chap who could throw six-inch nails better than some people could throw darts. Well here he is, Lew Walker from Gravesend, Kent. On 9 September 1984, in a seven hour non-stop marathon stint, Lew stuck 4,746 six-inch nails in the dartboard achieving a total score of 58,609. The total weight of nails thrown was 3 cwt 3 lb.

Dominoes

The longest recorded dominoes marathon was staged at St Anselm's College, Wirral, Merseyside, between 5 and 11 August 1985, when Neil Thomas and Tim Beesley played for 150 hr 5 min.

Knur and Spell

The aim of Knur and Spell is to knock an earthenware ball (or 'potty') from its

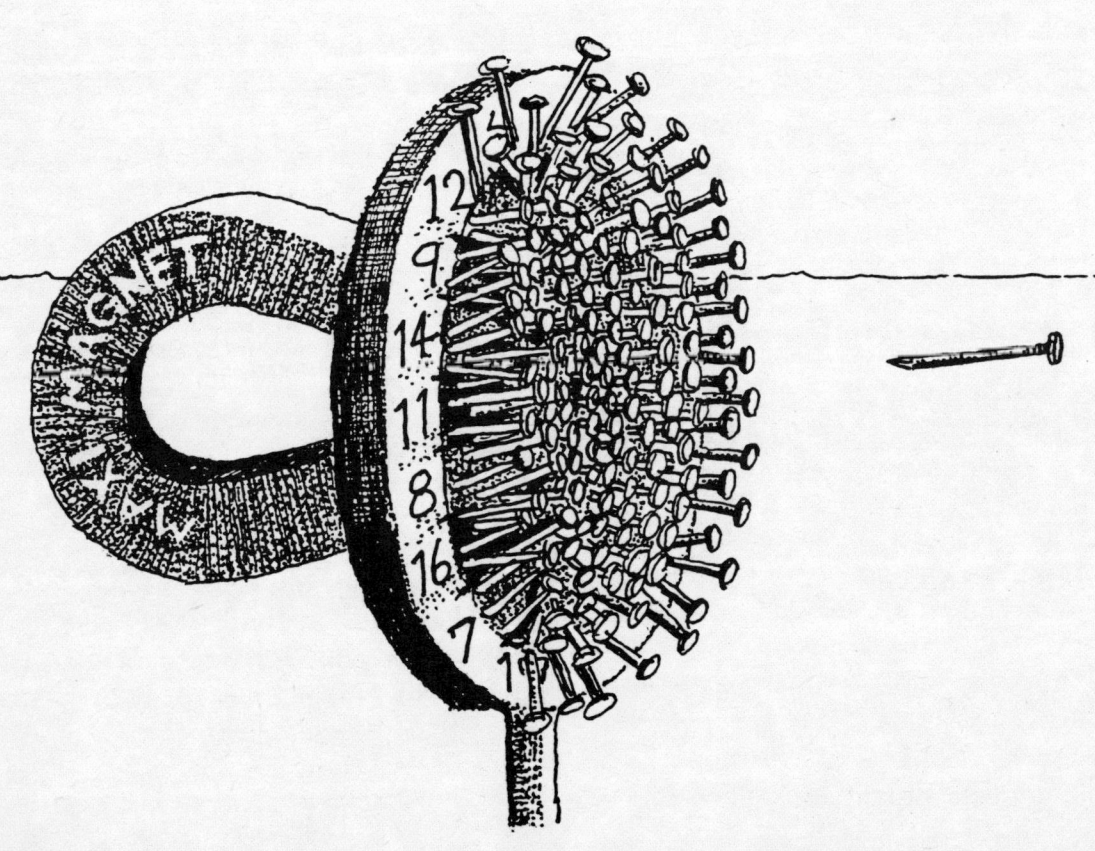

noose (the spell), using a long, club-like stick.

The longest distance that the 'potty' has been knocked is '15 score yards and 14 feet' – 304 yd 2 ft – by Joe Machin at The Queen's Ground, Barnsley, Yorkshire, in the season of 1899.

Match flicking

The greatest horizontal distance that anyone has flicked a standard 'lucifer' is 27 ft 4 in by Mike Barwell at the Royal British Legion Club, Hedon, Humberside, on 24 December 1981.

Nipsy

The longest recorded hit of a nipsy (a small piece of egg-shaped lignum vitae wood) is 208 yards by Joe Cooke of The Pheasant Inn, Monk Bretton, Barnsley, Yorkshire, at the Longfields, Darton, Yorkshire, during the 1962 season.

In the same season, Joe Cooke set another world record for nipsy by

achieving a total for his seven allowed hits of 1,064 yards.

Pinball marathon

From 2 to 4 March 1986 at The Shire Horse, Hull, Humberside, Terry Smith, 39, played pinball machines for a marathon 60 hours. During the record breaking stint, Terry used two machines, playing 1,034 games and notching up a total score of 420,434,445 points.

A team marathon of 100 hours was set by David Augustin, Geoffrey Newmarch, Malcolm Cook and Graham Migdalski, ending on 18th August 1973. All members used the same machine which could accommodate four players at a time.

Pool

According to reliable information, Michael Eufemia potted 625 consecutive balls in a ratified pool match series at Logans Billiard Academy, Brooklyn, New York, USA, on 2 February 1960.

The greatest number of balls pocketed in a 24 hour session is 15,780 by Victor Elliott at the Royal George, Lincoln, Lincolnshire, between 2 and 3 April 1985.

The longest marathon pool match ever played was one lasting 384 hr 3 min by Chris Pearman and Mark Lemm at the Crown, Horbury, Yorkshire, between 2 and 18 August 1984.

Pouff darts

The world pouff darts championships was last held in March 1938 at the Dorchester Hotel, London. Sponsored by the *Daily Mirror*, nine competitors took part and the eventual winner was Sidney Hall from Darlington, County Durham. Sidney was undefeated at the sport and on several occasions he held a dart crossways in his mouth and blew it accurately into a board from a distance of 28 feet.

Pub crawl – multi-county

The greatest number of British counties visited by way of imbibing at separate hostelries and inns (pub crawling) is 14 – Derbyshire, Warwickshire, Staffordshire, West Midlands, Hereford & Worcestershire, Gloucestershire, Oxfordshire, Buckinghamshire, Bedfordshire, Northamptonshire, Cambridgeshire, Lincolnshire, Leicestershire and Nottinghamshire. The time limit is set at the legal 5½ hours evening session and speed limits must be adhered to. The record was set on 21 December 1985 by Ranjit Johal, David Selvey, Patrick Bevan and Peter Gilbert.

Pub crawl – round Britain

The longest pub crawl ever attempted began at 5.35 pm on Friday 18 July 1986 at The Railway Inn, Saltash, Cornwall. From there the team of five – Ranjit Johal, Donald Smith, Patrick Bevan, David Selvey and Jacquie Lamb – visited one pub in every mainland county of Great Britain; all 62 of them. The crawl ended 76 hr 42 min later at the Bubble Inn, Stenson, Derbyshire, at 10.17 pm on Monday 21 July 1986.

Public house – longest name

It would appear that the 'landlords nouveaux' are creating 'battles royal' in order to attract more customers to their establishments. The latest craze is creating long names to get into the record books. By the time this book comes to print, I'm sure there will be a longer one, but for the time being the pub with the longest name is 'Henry J. Bean's (but his friends all call him Hank) Bar and Grill' sited in Raphael Street, London.

Public house – shortest name

The ultimate in short pub names is a record which can never be beaten. A pub owned by John Eales in Norfolk Crescent, Bayswater, London, is called ' '. No there's nothing missing, the pub doesn't have a name at all!

Public houses – most beers sampled

In a career spanning 16 years, George Morgan, 36, from Luton, Bedfordshire, claims to have visited 5,610 different pubs, sampling one pint of beer in each. By 1 January 1985, George had sampled 183 different types of draught beer and lager and 100 different types of bottled beers, lagers and stouts.

Rudest, crudest mine host

This category should attract a host of would-be claimants and nominees, but for the time being, the world's rudest, crudest and most fearsome mine host is 'Big Maggie' Rae, Landlady of Hic'ps Bar in Edinburgh, Scotland.

Maggie beat a host of other loathsome licensees in a contest run by Independent Television's 'TV AM'. In a career spanning 20 years, Maggie has tamed some of the roughest pubs in Edinburgh with the aid of 'Old Faithful' – a fearsome cudgel.

Smallest bar

The smallest bar in the world is the 'Phone Box Wine Bar' in the Huddersfield Hotel, Huddersfield,

Yorkshire. It is exactly as its name suggests – a phone box – and the licence was granted, despite objections from the Local Health Authority and Fire Officer, on 15 May 1985.

Table lifting

Using only a firm grip on one of the four supporting legs, Alan Pickering of Darlington, Cleveland, claims he can lift a 2 ft diameter bar table weighing 28 lbs to the vertical 20 times in one minute.

Extrovert record breaker Reg Morris always seems to make things more difficult for himself. He lifts pub tables too, but he lifts them with his teeth! On 2 September 1985 at the Royal Oak, Pelsall, West Midlands, Reg lifted a 28 lb pub table 20 times to the vertical in 1 min 30 sec, using only his teeth.

Reg also holds the world record for being the only person able to lift three pub tables simultaneously in his teeth, a feat involving a total weight of 84 lb.

Chapter Eight
'THE ALTERNATIVE OLYMPICS'

The first 'Alternative Olympics' took place at The Costello International Sports Stadium, Hull, Humberside, on 31 August 1986. And what a resounding success it was! The enthusiasm of the competitors was equally matched by that of the crowd and also the numerous local companies who sponsored individual disciplines by donations of money and equipment.

Originally it was planned that 'The Alternative Olympics' should be an annual event. However, because of the great number of potential entrants wishing to compete, it has been decided that the next Olympics will be in 1988. Major sponsors have been approached and judging by the response the next Olympics will be an international spectacular.

If you require an entry form, please write to me care of Grafton Books.

Teams from all parts of Britain assembled in Hull to take part, in particular an extremely strong team from Brentwood, Essex, who deservedly won several disciplines.

100 METRES CUSTARD FILLED WELLIES
1st	Patrick Howson	13.82 seconds*
2nd	Paul Smith	14.06 seconds
3rd	David Smith	14.55 seconds

PUDDING PLONKING
1st	David Pummell	103ft*
2nd	Julian Stevens	86 ft 6 in
3rd	David Whitecross	80 ft 8 in

GRAPE CATCHING
1st	Alan Peterson & Jane Whiteley	112 ft 4 in
2nd	John Davidson & Shaun Smith	110 ft 2 in
3rd	S. Ferguson & Harry Bennett	107 ft 2 in

100 METRES SPACE HOPPERS
1st	Darren Thomas	36.20 seconds
2nd	Edward Gardner	39.45 seconds
3rd	Pauline Bartholomew	40.31 seconds

HAGGIS HURLING
1st	David Pummel	134 ft 5 in
2nd	Shaun Barry	133 ft 8 in
3rd	David Smith	130 ft 3 in

500 METRES BEER CRATE RACE
1st	Paul Smith	1 min 31.70 sec*
2nd	Dave Stuart	1 min 50.31 sec
3rd	Nigel Wiseman	2 min 03.80 sec

100 METRE PEA PUSH
1st	David Armitage	11 min 14.30 sec
2nd	Anthony Pool	12 min 18.40 sec
3rd	Jonathan Rimmer	12 min 36.90 sec

BILLIARD CUE THROWING
1st	David Smith	116 ft 1 in*
2nd	Paul Smith	103 ft 3 in
3rd	Patrick Howson	99 ft 2 in

WATER-FILLED WELLY WANGING
1st	Stanley Bartle	14.90 metres
2nd	David Smith	14.87 metres
3rd	Mick Mullins	14.38 metres

ONE MILE PANTOMIME COW RACE
1st	Kevin Harris & Phil Clark	7 min 59.01 sec*
2nd	Rachel Lomotey & Rose Hutchinson	8 min 48.31 sec
3rd	Sue East & Liz Barkwith	8 min 59.60 sec

MOP BUCKET CARRYING (over distance of 50 ft)
1st	Brian Pratt	31*
2nd	David Smith	30
3rd	David Stewart	28

TYRE TOSSING
1st	Julian Stevens	13.30 metres*
2nd	David Smith	11.72 metres
3rd	Mick Mullins David Pummell	10.95 metres

ONE MILE CUSTARD-FILLED WELLIES
1st	Gary Spring	5 min 21.37 sec*
2nd	Derek Earl	5 min 27.89 sec
3rd	Tony Barkworth	5 min 40.72 sec

DRINKING LAGER THROUGH 4 MM STRAW
1st	Peter Dowdeswell	26.98 seconds*
2nd	Alex Liddle	27.74 seconds
3rd	John East	30.40 seconds

CREAM CRACKER (20) EATING
1st	John Smith	12 min 42.48 sec
2nd	Phil Clark	16 min 42.50 sec
3rd	David Whitecross	16 min 51.99 sec

*World Record

'Y FRONT' LEAPING (in one minute)
1st Stuart Cook   32*
2nd Kevin Harris   27
3rd Kerry McKinder   22

EATING 500 PEAS WITH COCKTAIL STICK
1st David Fulford   10 min 35.22 sec*
2nd Sally Ferguson   10 min 49.80 sec
3rd Kevin Holder   10 min 59.92 sec

BLACK PUDDING EATING
1st Steven Shand   3 lb in 15 min 17.2 sec
2nd Mick Mullins   3 lb in 21 min 53.7 sec
3rd Bruce Holdsworth   3 lb in 22 min 19.8 sec

ACKNOWLEDGEMENTS

I wish to extend my sincere thanks to the following for their help in researching this book:

Sir Cloughton Whitby, KBE
The Glenturret Distillery
Nick Lord, Brian Jones, John Fanshaw –
  Yorkshire Television
Mary O'Connell – BBC Television
The Independent Broadcasting Authority
C. Hartley – North West Lawn Mower Racing
  Association
Wilfred Makepeace Lunn
Several tins of Carlsberg Special Brew
Mirror Group Newspapers
The Daily Mail
The Daily Star
The Sun
The Weekly News
The Hull Daily Mail
Nick Cole – Scunthorpe Evening Telegraph

Peter Dowdeswell
Reg and Wendy Morris
Several more tins of Carlsberg Special Brew
Sue Barwell and Sandra Walton – typists
  extraordinaire

Also the following for their invaluable assistance at 'The Alternative Olympics':

Councillor John Ledger
The Hedon Scout Troup
David 'Crowley' Armitage
Kevin 'Dr Death' Holder
Stuart 'Bilbo' Patterson
Humberside Leisure Services
The Staff at Costello Sports Stadium
Steve King and Eric the Viking – Viking Radio
Sue Barwell
Joshua Tetley & Son Ltd